Lost Generation?

Also available from Continuum

Overschooled but Undereducated, John Abbot, Heather MacTaggart and Prue Leith
Killing Thinking, Mary Evans

Lost Generation?

New strategies for youth
and education

MARTIN ALLEN AND
PATRICK AINLEY

continuum

Continuum International Publishing Group
The Tower Building   80 Maiden Lane, Suite 704
11 York Road   New York, NY 10038
London SE1 7NX

www.continuumbooks.com

British Library Cataloguing-in-Publication Data
A catalogue record for this book is available from the British Library.

ISBN: 9781441134707 (paperback)

Library of Congress Cataloging-in-Publication Data

Allen, Martin, 1955-

Lost generation? : new strategies for youth and education /
    Martin Allen and Patrick Ainley.
p. cm.

Includes bibliographical references and index.

ISBN 978-1-4411-3470-7 (pbk.)

1. Education–Economic aspects–Great Britain. 2. Youth–
    Employment–Great Britain. 3. Labor supply–Effect
    of education on–Great Britain. 4. School-to-work
    transition–Great Britain. I. Ainley, Patrick. II. Title.
LC67.G7A45 2010
338.4'7370941–dc22

Typeset by Pindar NZ, Auckland, New Zealand
Printed and bound in Great Britain by the MPG Books Group

Contents

Acknowledgements

Matthew Cheeseman for the many suggestions he made, only some of which we have been able to add – we should have talked to him sooner as he probably knows more about English under-graduate experience than anyone else no longer living it. Lorraine Petersen for also kindly reading the draft all through – any remaining errors are not her responsibility. Also, other students and former-students at the University of Greenwich and elsewhere – including on Facebook – who have shared their opinions and experiences with us. Beulah and Adam.

My sixth-form economics students and their efforts to make sense of the current global crisis. Colleagues and comrades in the National Union of Teachers. To J for curiosity and providing a different take. To friends, family and, in particular, a teenager, or two.

Introduction

New term, September 2009

No one would seriously claim that the rush of applicants for UK university and college places in summer 2009 represented a new found enthusiasm amongst the nation's youth for higher learning. Nor that it was the triumphant achievement of the New Labour government's long-held goal for half of 18–30 year olds to be in some sort of higher education by 2010. In fact, the government had refused to fund the necessary increase in places and was later to fine those institutions that offered them.

Nor could it be claimed that the record levels of qualification of the applicants for undergraduate degrees that reached unprecedented proportions of top passes (67.1per cent A-C at A-level) – represented a new accumulation of knowledge or wisdom when the publication of rising GCSE and A-level scores and their Scots equivalents are annually dismissed by a media chorus with the insensitive label of 'dumbing down'. Indeed, grade inflation is recognised by all but government, university Vice Chancellors and the heads of exam boards. These are the same vested interests for whom the queues of would-be students willing to pay, only encouraged those in the elite universities who want to raise fees still higher – perhaps to whatever the market will bear.

It is surely not coincidental that widespread allegations of 'diploma devaluation' coincided with widening participation to post-compulsory further and higher education and accompanied supposedly rising standards in compulsory schooling. This paradox is explored and explained in this book. Similarly, social mobility is known to have decreased at the same time as participation has been widened to higher education. There are also considerable doubts about whether levels of non-computer literacy and numeracy have risen at all. A generation of students and teachers at school, college and university are working harder, but not necessarily learning more.

Another paradox whose resolution is also becoming clear to the growing number of disillusioned educators and educated alike, is that in important respects, society is not learning at all but the culture becoming more ignorant and irrational. It is not just that teaching to tests may not, after all, have improved literacy and numeracy when student standards of spelling and maths are slipping. More importantly, largely corporately owned mass media daily plumb new depths of banality and sensation, whilst a self-destructive society is stuck in recession and slides towards ecological catastrophe. This is perhaps the gravest indictment that can be made of the education system since the prime role of institutionalised learning in any society should be to critically learn from the past to discover new knowledge that can contribute to altering social behaviour in the future.

Hope triumphed over experience in the willingness of would-be students to rack up record debts for student fees and loans in expectation that they would be repaid with professional salaries in three or more years' time. The experience this ignored was that of those graduating a few months earlier in record numbers to another media chorus greeting them as 'the lost generation' of graduates without jobs. They were the first to have paid the new higher fees and therefore left higher education with record levels of debt. The desperate hope of many of the new applicants and their parents – along with other not so young people who also applied – was that the economy would soon recover from the recession into which it had plunged the year before and business as usual would soon be resumed, a bandwagon joined often by pure panic at the lack of any other alternative.

Overtested and undereducated

To understand how this situation came about, our first chapter recounts the history of education and training in England since the war. To do this it compresses the account we presented in our 2007 book *Education make you fick, innit?* which was written mainly for Education Studies students but is here précised for a more general readership. We move on from the past to the middle three chapters which look at the present before advancing an alternative future in the last chapter.

Chapter 2 then looks at the testing regime that has been imposed on England's schools and colleges and which is now sinking under its own weight. We explain how and why this is happening and we look at its consequences which are endemic to the whole system of education and training. One consequence is the culture of plagiarism shared across education. Another is that competition between schools, parents and students has generated a new cramming industry of private tuition on and off line, adding to the national obsession with passing tests and taking exams.

We also explain how it happened that under New Labour, while being 'over tested' and assessed as never before, many young people, despite their prolonged period in formal education, can also be considered 'undereducated'. For the large majority of students – and their teachers who, instead of being autonomous professionals, have become the directed deliverers of a product – education has become a mechanical and instrumental affair. Students learn what they have to, when they have to and in many cases by whatever means they have to. The perception of this situation is not lost upon them, as a final year Education Studies student at the University of Greenwich summarised in his investigation project in 2004:

> Students learn to connect their self esteem and what they may achieve in later life to their exam results . . . Over-assessment has made subject knowledge and understanding a thing of the past as students are put through a routine year after year, practising what exactly to write and where in preparation for exams.

The traditionally English system of selectivity in education now goes on much longer so that it stretches from primary to postgraduate school. Just as at the end of the nineteenth century, teaching to the test dominates classrooms, often for weeks, months or even terms at a time and then the cycle starts again. This has ingrained feelings of insecurity in parents, teachers and students alike.

Overqualified and underemployed

Our third chapter confronts the economic realities to show how the recession has intensified longer term changes in the relationship between education qualifications and the labour market. Even if there is a partial recovery, there will be a ratchet effect which will raise the bar to worthwhile employment at the same time as qualification inflation continues to devalue all qualifications with the effect that participating in education is like running up a down escalator. Rather than the endless opportunities offered by the 'knowledge economy', for many young people – even many of those with qualifications – casualised, low-wage, contract and unskilled jobs are increasingly the only ones available; if they can find those! So, the argument in this book is that any increase in 'high skilled' and well-remunerated professional and managerial employment has not been able to absorb the increase in the level of educational credentials held by the population. The corollary is that people are overqualified for most jobs that remain.

Nevertheless, a further complication is that – despite this situation – talk about 'skill' has become ubiquitous as the word has lost any definite sense (Warhurst et al. 2004). Skill in its traditional craft meaning has been systematically dismantled over the last 30 years with the growth of services and the way new information and computing technology has been applied in employment. As we also suggest, this process of deskilling is now reaching up the employment hierarchy to reduce many non-manual so-called professional and 'middleclass' occupations to the level of wage labour, ie. to jobs, not salaried careers with security. Simultaneously, occupations calling themselves 'professional' have grown with the expansion of services and non-manual office work. Thus, rather than education professionalising the proletariat, there has been an actual proletarianisation of the professions.

Just as 'skills talk' is ubiquitous, so governments have been reiterating 'education, education, education' even before 'Education' became, in Blair's words again, 'our most important economic policy'. Now the contending mainstream political parties are at it again. In the run up to a general election and desperate to find the money to continue to bankroll its policies, though pledging to defend 'front line' services, Labour advances more of the same. Conservatives however champion a return to traditional academic values. As Tory education minister, Gove may make a virtue of vouchers for schools and a free market in student fees.

The repetition and unreality of this 'Great Debate on Education', echoing on from its tedious original in 1976, is an even clearer sign than the 2009 MPs' 'expenses scandal', of the bankruptcy of what the media call 'the political class'. This is actually a crisis of the new market-state that was introduced under Mrs Thatcher's premiership in a desperate response to the crisis of the post-war welfare state. Now that crisis solution has ended in what Andy Haldane, Executive Director for Financial Stability at the Bank of England, admitted was 'the largest and most synchronous global economic slowdown since the Great Depression' (*Society Now* 2009). In this book we show how the education and training system of the 1980s pioneered new market-state relations that turned citizens into consumers. Both education and the market-state face a renewed questioning of their legitimacy but retain it because of the lack of any coherent alternative.

These developments have all been accentuated by the recession which has seen an unemployment level for 16–24 year olds already close to a million; estimates vary between one in five and one in four of the age group. From being a minority 'hard core' intent on bucking the system, the category of NEET ('Not in employment, education or training') now represents up to 17 per cent of 16–24 year olds. The 'lost generation' label that the media initially applied to graduates without jobs generally disregarded this larger lost generation of the majority simultaneously leaving school or college for apprenticeships or other supposedly 'vocational' training without jobs. They are in competition with the older unemployed being forced into the same *Poor Work*, as Brown and Scase called it in 1991. Meanwhile snobbery, racism and sexism permeate an educational hierarchy that completely mirrors the class structure of society topped by its leading fee-paying private schools and ancient universities.

Everyone knows but few admit that the largely literary abilities assessed by tests in schools and academic examinations for higher education are proxies for what the French sociologist of education, Pierre Bourdieu, called 'cultural capital'. This in turn is a proxy for the real money capital that can afford to purchase it in the most academically prestigious institutions. Certainly, all teachers know that, as Martell wrote in 1976, 'As you move down the socio-economic class scale, kids read and write less well' (107). So this ordering of levels of literacy by the apparently most unbiased and academic of assessments reproduces the structures of wealth and privilege in society.

'Old mole'

It is also rarely acknowledged that the endless chatter about education actually masks, but is another way of talking about, social class. Particularly that old mole of English society, the working class, has been transformed since the collapse of industrial employment in the 1970s, following which both Conservative and New Labour governments claimed to have educated it out of existence. Prime Minister Major for example, announced Britain had become a classless society whilst his successor Blair declared 'the class war is over' – although he did not tell us who won! Even as 'classism' joined racism and sexism as socially unacceptable, Blair and his successor Brown continued to insist that there was 'more room at the top' for those who were well qualified, while those at the bottom had only themselves to blame for not taking advantage of the opportunities for education and training that an 'enabling state' made available to them.

In Chapter 3 we examine how the class structure has changed, or rather, how class has been recomposed. Education and training have influenced and in turn been affected by this on-going process of class recomposition. With the decline of manufacturing industry, the traditional manual/ non-manual division has been eroded. However, in place of an expanding middleclass – reflecting upward mobility – the majority of the population sits uneasily within a new 'working middle' of society as the class structure has turned pear shaped. Rather than becoming an agent of social mobility, educational qualifications have become the main source of 'social' and 'cultural capital', providing for their holders a gateway into the more secure and privileged sections of the occupational hierarchy. As more of the population have become 'better educated' – or at least more highly qualified, there has been an increasingly desperate scramble for places in 'good schools'. These elite schools, sixth-form colleges and universities invariably argue that they are 'maintaining standards,' even 'rescuing scholarship', as they have sought to distinguish themselves by offering new and more academic qualifications. Or, in the case of parts of higher education, by insisting that they are allowed to charge higher fees to ensure that they remain 'world class'.

The escalating cost of a university education combined with worsening employment opportunities and increased accommodation costs as part of the overall housing crisis. This has resulted, we suggest in Chapter 4, in new forms of dependency by young people on their parents. Remaining at home until well into one's twenties is now commonplace, leading us to suggest that rather than the transition to adulthood being more 'prolonged' than in the post-war years, many young people, will never be able to grow up at all in the sense of becoming independent of their parents and/or the state. Chapter 4 also compares the situation post-18 of students with that of non-students and between different types of students. It asks if these are one undifferentiated mass of individuals who are all more or less 'lost'? Or, even if divided one from another by an education system that only confirms and emphasizes the social differences between them, could they not also find interests in common?

New strategies for youth and education

As education and training, if not 'lifelong learning', has intruded into the lives of more and more people – not just the young who are the most schooled and tested of any generation ever – media obsession with aspects of education follows the unprecedented primacy education has taken in successive governments' policies. Yet what is the purpose of institutionalised learning for a society that prepares for its own future through so much emphasis upon 'Learning unto death', as Glenn Rikowski called it in 1999? This is *The Youth Question* that Phil Cohen rethought in 1997: how society integrates the new generations into its on-going structures in order to maintain itself by making the future resemble the past. In Chapter 5 we aim to take Cohen's rethinking further in the unique circumstances of a new century. The President of the Royal Society (Rees 2003), a highly respected scientific authority, has written that we may well soon be witnessing the termination of humanity if coordinated international action is not taken urgently to alter our social trajectory by making the future very different from the recent past. In which case the 'lost generation' might also be the last generation!

So this is not just another book on education and training, but one that reaches wider to confront the situation of the new generation in what will be their twenty-first century. What education can best prepare them for it? Surely not the one we currently inflict upon them! Already the young generation is unique in being the most rigorously tested ever. They are also smaller as a proportion of the population than the older generation that got them into the situation in which they find themselves. As the next generation of adults they are likely to be significantly less wealthy than their predecessors. This deprivation does not fall evenly however. Confronting it collectively will require major changes in learning at all levels.

To begin with there needs to be a radically different approach to the curriculum. There is no going back to what the elitists consider to be the 'good old days' when education was designed for a minority and examinations selected a few. We argue for a 'really useful' education, one that breaks down divisions between what is currently referred to as 'academic' and 'vocational' learning; but also for an education that empowers people, encouraging them to realise that, rather than being its passive victims, they can take control of economy and society.

The style of this book

This is not an 'academic' book – at least in the way that term is conventionally used. As we contend in Chapter 4, much academic social research has not been able to keep up with the changes in education and the lives of young people. Rather than addressing the big picture, it is often small scale; intensive and revealing though this can be, it not unusually devotes as much attention to justifying its methodology as it does to explaining its results. Moreover, the process of academic research involves a long process of bidding for funding (usually unsuccessfully – initially at least), then of implementing and writing up. By the time it appears – in journals that also take months at best to review and publish the material – findings can be only of historical interest.

In comparison, this book was written over a relatively brief period when the short comings of New Labour's economic and education policies were laid bare. While referring to academic work, it also relies on newspaper and online media sources, but also considers findings from commercial market research since big business continues to regard young people as important customers. The book tries to make itself accessible to practitioners who, increasingly sapped of energy, have little time to read. Even academics who see themselves as progressive often only reinforce the Chinese wall between theory and practice or between what Italian communist leader, Antonio Gramsci, referred to as 'organic intellectuals' and the masses. In any case, to secure an academic career articles in prestigious journals are preferred to books.

So, while we write principally for students and teachers at all levels of learning and focus primarily on education, since this has come to play such a large part in the lives of most (young) people today, we intend to appeal to all who work or are involved in any capacity with young people, whether as parents or carers, youth workers and social workers of all sorts, or just as proverbial concerned citizens. We also recognise that, inevitably, thanks in large part to the continuing and possibly worsening inadequacies of the education system, there are many people about whom this book is written who will never get the chance to read it. Sadly, until education is organised differently, this is always likely to be the case.

Teachers and lecturers remain crucial to the construction of an alternative education. Unlike their students who enter a situation they are likely to accept as given and some of their younger colleagues who have never experienced anything different, the incremental changes of the past 30 years and more have crept upon too many involved in education unawares. In particular, learning has been so confused with assessment that many in schools, colleges and universities are unable any longer to distinguish between them. Snake-oil solutions based on neuro-myths abound: from 'brain gym' in primary schools to spurious 'learning styles' dividing students in new ways up through further and higher education (Coffield et al. 2004, Harari 2005).

A sense of pointlessness is pervasive. Even as parents are assured by the Inspectorate that record results have been achieved by the most professional teachers ever, at the same time probationary years are extended with demands for more tests to weed out incompetents. Ground down by ever more exacting demands, one sector of education blames another – higher blames secondary, secondary blames primary, while all disparage further education. Academics in elite universities default to a defence of traditional standards, while in education departments those whose courses of teacher education have given way to training in government-dictated competences have least to say. They are no longer able within the constrictions placed upon them to convey any larger sense of the context of pedagogy.

Many teachers yearn for a return to their old 'professionalism' but we argue that this expertise – as we see it – needs to be redefined. This is necessary to create a new learning consensus with students, particularly those students in their upper secondary years and beyond who, instead of being able to complete their education, have accepted that they will remain as indebted full-time learners way beyond the compulsory leaving age. In short, we advocate a new educational politics which, while allowing teachers and other workers to develop their expertise, also 'brings young people back in' and goes beyond simply changing what is taught to address issues of democracy.

Looking at the system as a whole

Uniquely this book engages with education and training as a whole to include schools, colleges and universities. This is because you cannot understand what is going on by dealing with it piecemeal and examining each sector separately as most education studies do. We combine our experience to integrate compulsory schooling with post-compulsory further, higher, adult education and training. This includes formal and informal learning inside and outside education institutions since we have to look also at the larger experience of successive generations. Coming of age in society today is very different to previous post-war experiences and it may no longer be possible to impose old policy models upon it or even to think about it in familiar ways.

Certainly, without a holistic view we maintain that it is impossible to understand what has happened to education in recent years. If they are lost in the system, the only way students and their teachers can begin to find their way out of it is by understanding its workings as a totality. This will help them to recover the sense of purpose and worth – if not professional status – that teachers in schools, colleges and universities have lost. Similarly, students can overcome the alienation induced by institutionalised learning today.

As long as they do not succumb to depressing feelings of personal inadequacy, young people are not 'lost'. As a recently received email from a former student puts it, 'I feel my life is on a standstill and that is annoying me'. Many feel similarly but their anger is so far directed into a determination to succeed as individuals in the competition for the remaining jobs. So they are 'trapped' or 'stuck' perhaps, but not without individual and collective agency and the intelligence to find their way out of their situation aided by the teachers who are their natural allies. Alongside others working with them, including their parents or carers but also youth and community workers of all sorts, this book is intended to help all of us cut through the stock responses and repetitive justifications for things as they are. It suggests that education at all levels can be claimed for its true purpose of social enlightenment and help find a new direction for society.

1

From Jobs without Education to Education without Jobs

Introduction

The new secondary state education system was the proudest component of the welfare state established by the Labour government
after the war, second only to the National Health Service. It was
subsequently endorsed and expanded by successive Conservative
administrations. The 1944 Education Act and the reforms that
later followed are widely seen as major steps towards improving
opportunities for children and young people. Even if the post-war
tripartite system of grammar, technical and secondary modern
schools preserved gross inequalities between classes, genders and
later between different ethnic groups, these reforms should never
be underestimated.

The Education Bill presented to Parliament in the winter of 1943
by a Conservative Education Minister, removed the distinction
between elementary and secondary education to abolish fee paying
in all state-maintained secondary schools. The school leaving age
was raised to 15 in 1947. The comprehensive reform of secondary
schools followed after 1965, together with a more child-centred
primary education and the expansion of further, higher and adult
education. Together these constituted what Phil Mizen calls a new
'Keynesian state of youth' (2004: 17). The baby boom generation
was thus one of the biggest beneficiaries of post-war reconstruction.

However, while clearly important, the direct influence of state
schooling on the lives of many working-class young people during

this period needs to be kept in proper perspective. Until the mid 1970s, the majority of the children of the industrial working class, then forming the majority of the population, left school without any real qualifications and only basic education. Universal literacy, for example, was never attained (then or since) and schooling did not enjoy anywhere near the degree of 'hegemony' or ideological influence over young people's lives that it does today. The extent to which compulsory education was, or ever can be, 'popular' (CCCS 1981), as opposed to oppressively dominating young people's experience (as it does today), is a question we pursue throughout this book.

Tripartism

The language of the 1944 Act was clear in its conception of three different types of children for whom three distinct types of schooling were appropriate. Of course, the incoming Labour administration emphasised the 'parity of esteem' between grammar, technical and secondary modern schools but this was contradicted by the pre-war Norwood Report on which the Act was based. This had outlined three distinct types of minds naturally, genetically inherited in a ratio of 20:40:40. These were 'first class minds . . . interested in learning for its own sake' who needed to remain in education for longest; secondly, those for whom 'the subtleties of language construction are too delicate' but who could apply knowledge practically; finally, those 'below average . . . whose future employment will not demand any measure of technical skill or knowledge', as Norwood explained (HMSO 1943: 201). Psychometricians claimed these invariant 'Intelligence Quotients' could be scientifically measured by an IQ test to match the minds of eleven year olds to secondary schooling appropriate for their future employment.

At a time of labour shortages raising the school leaving age was opposed by many employers but the different types of state schools for these three different kinds of minds happily coincided with the divisions of knowledge and labour in traditional heavy industry reconstructed after the war. These separated non-manual professional and managerial occupations from skilled and 'unskilled' manual workers. Like the division of the men of gold, silver and bronze in Plato's *Republic*, this corresponded in turn with the established order of middle, respectable and rough working classes.

The upper or ruling class tended to disappear from this conventional class pyramid, like their private schools. These were 'shunted', as the architect of the Act, R.A. Butler, recalled of 'the first class carriage . . . onto an immense siding' (1971: 120) and more or less forgotten about thereafter. Although catering for only 7per cent of young people (a figure that has remained remarkably constant until recently), the continuing dominance and influence of these private elite schools over the state education system was maintained through their close links with the antique universities and their exam boards. In the absence of any National Curriculum, they dictated the syllabuses of academic examinations, like the A-levels established in 1951 and taken by grammar-school pupils who stayed on post-15 to enter sixth form.

Arguably, other aspects of post-war reconstruction were more significant than the new secondary schools in achieving a new settlement between the state and post-war generations. Most important was a government commitment to maintain 'full employment'. Consequently, post-war economic expansion ensured that wages increased significantly and job opportunities were plentiful in most parts of England and young people were the main beneficiaries in terms of employment opportunities. In the post-war period, as Mizen shows, youth was subject to an 'extensive process of reorganisation' (2004: 17). The mass of youth for the first time was recognised as a distinct section of the population, despite the way that Gill Jones, in her book on *Youth* records:

> the welfare state, based on age thresholds, effectively standardized the life course into three phases, of education (childhood), work (adulthood) and rest (old age), thus accentuating the differences between these states rather than the relationships between them. (2009: 89)

Youth and (non-statutory) youth provision fitted uneasily into the brief period between the immature 'dependence' of childhood and the mature 'independence' of adulthood. This was marked not only by a wage but definitively by independently maintaining 'dependents' in a family of your own.

Young women were encouraged to marry early 'to replenish the stock of the race' after the losses of war – as William Beveridge, key founder of the welfare state, put it. Many young working-class male school-leavers entered apprenticeships. A high point of 25 per cent of young workers – mainly boys – were apprenticed in 1969 (FECRDU 1978: 34–5). Most school leavers headed for unskilled work however and found they had little trouble getting it. In most parts of the country they were also able to move easily from one job to another; half changed jobs within a year and a fifth changed jobs 'frequently' (Finn 1987: 47). Persistent labour shortages meant young people's wages rose to unprecedented heights, especially as apprenticeship regulations were tightened after the war by new legislation limiting the number of hours young people could work (Finn: 45). Even without legal prescription, along with non-statutory adult, careers and youth services, the number of newly designated 'further education' colleges also doubled after the war.

Further Education colleges, developed from existing Local Authority technical and adult institutes, took up the slack when the technical schools promised by the 1944 Act did not materialise in many areas. This left a binary system of grammar and secondary modern state schools rather than the tripartite one that was originally planned. As a result, for many young people, day release courses in the new colleges constituted their first real experience of technical education. However, until the 1970s almost half of all boys and most girls continued to enter jobs where no formal training or additional education was provided or required. So much so that the National Youth Employment Council recorded in 1974:

> Careers Officers find it easy to help pupils from Educationally Subnormal schools because they come out better equipped to face the world and tackle a job of work than pupils from the lower streams of comprehensive and modern schools. (37)

Post-war sociologists provided extensive evidence of how working-class students were failing to match the performance of their middleclass counterparts in the state school system, so again leaving the private schools largely out of account. One of the most eminent educationalists, Basil Bernstein (1971), proposed that education alone could never 'compensate' for wider inequalities in society; while Jackson and Marsden (1962) described the humiliations working-class children endured in grammar schools, not only from other pupils but also from staff. Working-class opposition to compulsory schooling was such that Paul Willis suggested, rather than being failed by the school system, many working-class kids failed themselves to follow peers and relatives onto the factory shop floor (Willis 1977: 1). It was, Willis suggested, their own culture rather than the state's education system – as other Marxist writers maintained (eg. Bowles and Gintis 1976 in the USA) – that reproduced class inequalities. Instead of the school system preparing them for subordinate roles within the labour process, Willis's 'lads' prepared themselves. Even in the early 1970s, 40per cent of young people left school without any qualifications. Many, as Willis described, had at school made use only of opportunities for 'havin a laff' at their teachers' expense, especially the ones who tried to engage with them.

By contrast, qualifications and staying on beyond the statutory school-leaving age predominated only amongst the growing middleclass. They made what established itself over the post-war decades as an institutionalised transition from school to white-collar and professional careers in the expanding welfare state at the same time as moving from home to living away via higher education. They were joined in HE by the small minority of working-class students who had passed the 11+ to achieve social mobility via grammar schools at a time when 'meritocracy' had some meaning. As in the USA, 'so-called social mobility was a product of the specific conditions of economic development at a particular time' (Aronowitz 2008: 20–1). This period came to an end coincident with, but not, it can be emphasised, as a consequence of the introduction of comprehensive schools. As a result, meritocracy then was more than the code word for the 'individualistic and competitive values promoted by New Labour' that Angela McRobbie (2009: 209) describes it as having become today.

Comprehensive reforms

Neither was the move towards comprehensive schooling as universal as is sometimes implied. Although Harold Wilson's Labour government returned to office in 1964 committed to comprehensive reform, it did not attempt to legislate as DES circular 10/65 only 'requested' Local Authorities to submit plans for reform. So on the ground, comprehensivisation remained incomplete and where structural change took place it was not matched by curricular reform. This left the new comprehensives competing for exam success with the established private and surviving grammar schools – 'grammar schools for all', as the 1964 election Manifesto had promised. Benn and Chitty in their 1996 review optimistically reported good progress in the comprehensive reform of up to 80 per cent of all English state secondary schools (more in Wales and Scotland but not until later in Northern Ireland). Despite this, grammar schools continue to exist in many areas and the 'hidden' selection, which continued in many schools that were comprehensive in name only, has now become universal.

Of course, there were particular advances. Even if moves towards less hierarchical and more mixed ability methods of teaching were hardly encouraged by the inherited academic curriculum, a committed minority of teachers tried to build more creative and more egalitarian relationships with their students. Many of the courses set up for those in their later years, like the teacher-marked and moderated CSE mode 3s in the 1970s, allowed more constructive classroom engagements. They were deliberately 'student centred' rather than academically subject-centred. Several new courses, like the 'New Social Studies' (Lawton and Dufour 1973), included more controversial content and encouraged discussion of radical ideas (Jones 1983). A network of initiatives emerged; in particular, the Schools Council Humanities Project and Nuffield Science, not to mention alternative approaches to the teaching of English and maths.

More radical was the journal *Teaching London Kids* which challenged not only traditional subject hierarchies but also the power structure of schools themselves. In higher education as well, a new sociology of education developed, along with sociology itself and combined courses in the new polytechnics and universities. The new sociologists of education were critical of 'deficit' explanations of working-class failure at school. They encouraged trainee teachers to discover the politics behind the school curriculum (Young and Whitty 1976). In primary schools the 1967 Plowden Report emphasised a more child-centred approach based on the individual growth of each child and in 1978 the Warnock Report extended the comprehensive project to children with redefined Special Educational Needs.

Similarly in post-compulsory education, the 1963 Robbins Report rejected the idea of a fixed 20 per cent 'pool' of intelligence and recommended expansion of higher education to 'all who could benefit from it'. Along with technical colleges elevated to university status, new universities were built on the edge of Cathedral towns around the country. But the model that had become established for middleclass youth, making a transition to work and independent living via campus-based university/ finishing school, was not extended to the working-class. Instead, new urban polytechnics provided local degree-level higher education often linked to employment. These became home to many of the former teacher training colleges where new education degrees and post-graduate certification charged radicalised graduates with enthusiasm for teaching.

Again though, the influence of these changes on classroom life for the majority of teachers and students should not be over-emphasized. In 1972 the extension of compulsory secondary schooling by the raising of the school leaving age was opposed by many working-class students and their parents (Finn 1987, Willis 1977). They were keen that they should 'get out and earn some money' and ROSLA was widely seen as a way of disguising rising youth unemployment. We would not denigrate education reforms made in the name of working-class children but we should recognise that for many, 'secondary education for all' – whether comprehensive or not – still represented a diversion more than an entitlement. In this respect, and despite the 1964 Industrial Training Act that levied employers to subsidise apprenticeships and technical training in colleges, it is appropriate to refer to this period as one when most young people left school for 'jobs without education'.

Leaving school and starting work, leaving home and getting married

In the post-war period, 'leaving school for work' was eagerly anticipated by many young people – not only Willis's 'lads'. As Michael Anderson noted in 1983, during the 1960s a 14–15 year-old:

> could with reasonable probability of being right, have predicted within a few years the timing of his or her future life course – leaving school, entering employment, leaving home, marrying and setting up home, early patterns of child-bearing and rearing. (13)

Though traditional industries were in terminal decline, recruitment patterns were maintained. For instance, in their classic 1961 study of the working-class community of Bethnal Green, Wilmott and Young described the importance of relatives 'speaking for' young men to ensure their employment in local industries; while Dennis et al. (1957) documented continuity of employment across generations in the mining industry and similarly Carter (1962) in the then booming steel town of Sheffield. Boys in particular would make a 'collective transition' when they left school with their 'mates', continuing to work with them in the manufacturing, construction or primary sector of the economy.

Comparing patterns of leaving home in the early 1990s, Jones (1995: 23) notes that transitions from youth to adulthood during the 1950s and 1960s:

> certainly appear to be at their most condensed, most coherent and most unitary. Many young adults, especially those from working-class families, left home, married and started families within a short space of time.

The average age of first marriage for women recorded its lowest post-war point of 20 (22 for men) in the 1971 census. Its rise over just three decades to 28.2 (30.5 for men) indicates the huge changes in gender relations and in family formation that have taken place.

One often-noted effect of the long period of economic prosperity after the war was the flourishing of new types of youth consumerism. Despite its eulogised male manifestations from the 1950s teddy boys on, this was pioneered largely by the buying power of teenage working-class girls. The rebellious 'rituals' of the new 'youth cultures' and their disdain for many aspects of established authority reflected deeper contradictions and inequalities experienced by different sections of youth (Hall and Jefferson 1976). They shocked the generation of adults emerging from years of war-time austerity but their immense creativity, augmented by a new generation of post-war immigrants from Britain's former-colonies, contributed to a popular cultural renaissance in the 1960s expressed most vividly through music, dance and dress.

1970–80s: Training without jobs

The improved economic position of many young people during a period described by historian Eric Hobsbawm (1995: 257) as 'the golden years' of British capitalism – 'the thirty glorious years' as they call them in France – went into reverse from the mid-1970s when an economic downturn intensified longer term changes in the labour market and sent unemployment soaring. After averaging about 1.5 per cent during the 1960s (though higher in the North, Scotland and Wales and never under 7 per cent in Northern Ireland – even higher in Catholic areas), unemployment increased to over 4 per cent by mid-1975. Mrs Thatcher finally abandoned government commitment to full employment in 1979, following the previous Labour government's unofficial acceptance of this condition for an IMF loan in 1976. As Elliot and Atkinson record (2007: 31):

> The first decision taken by the new Chancellor, Sir Geoffrey Howe, was to abolish exchange controls, the means by which governments of both left and right had, since the Second World War, sought to . . . sustain full employment.

During Thatcher's monetarist experiment at the beginning of the 1980s, 40,000 people were joining the dole queue each month and unemployment passed three million to reach over 11 per cent of the workforce by 1985. After a temporary recovery, it again reached almost 10 per cent in the early 1990s. Just as in the preceding Lawson boom, during New Labour's consumer boom the Labour Force Survey (generally considered more accurate than the government's Claimant Count), showed that the 'full employment' government claimed was never really restored. Instead, growing job insecurity for those who were employed was combined with an expanding periphery of contract workers, ducking and diving at two or three part-time and temporary jobs simultaneously.

If young people had benefited from economic expansion, with stagnation they became one of the groups to suffer most. The Industrial Training Boards with their levy-grant system for employers were wound up from 1972 and ever since successive repetitive debates over education and training have sought a replacement for the apprenticeships that were lost. As the 1970s progressed, figures for youth unemployment continued to surpass those for adults and by 1986 it was estimated that more than half of 16 and 17 year olds (Finn 1987: 187) and a quarter of 18 and 19 year olds were unemployed (Mizen 2004: 55). This created, Dorling (2010) emphasizes, the first or original post-war 'lost generation'.

However, it was the 'deficiencies' of young people themselves, unable to make the 'transition to independence' and blamed for their continued 'dependence' on the state and their families that were presented as contributing to their condition – rather than the lack of any employment for them. Their schools and teachers were also blamed as working-class youth were identified in 1976 by James Callaghan, the last Old Labour Prime Minister, as poorly skilled and educated and so a centralised system of 'youth training' was introduced to compensate for 'failing' comprehensive schools.

The alternative recommended by the 1979 Macfarlane Report of developing tertiary colleges was rejected by the incoming Thatcher government. The door was thus closed on a national extension of comprehensive secondary provision to a tertiary level with a vocational and academic, full and part-time integrated course offer for all school leavers (see Simmons 2009). Instead, the grammar/ private school ethos of academic sixth forms was preserved for a minority.

The majority of school leavers in the 1980s ended up on a succession of Youth Training Schemes (YTS) run by the Manpower Services Commission (MSC), an off-shoot of the Department of Employment. Rather than being closed down by the Conservatives as they had promised in the 1979 election, this was the first of many central government non-departmental public bodies (as they are now called) and it played a growing role in the lives of school leavers (Ainley and Corney 1990). It pioneered, particularly in training and FE where it made its first inroads, a new 'public management' borrowed from the private sector in which central government agencies contract out funding to public and private institutions competing with each other for students and bidding to tender other services. Supposedly 'freeing' institutional leaders from the vested interests of local council and civil service bureaucracies, this new market way of organising the state creates new layers of bureaucracy and inspection as power contracts to the centre while responsibility for meeting targets is contracted out to agents for delivery.

Using these methods, in 1977 the MSC bypassed the Local Authorities to offer training places to a quarter of a million 16–19 year olds. By 1983 over three million were signed up for YTS, often run by the private employers and other agencies the state subsidised. Supposedly these schemes offered a 'bridge' from school to work by developing the new 'transferable skills' that, it was claimed, were now needed in the modern workplace. The theory was that 'counter-cyclical training' would prepare the new workforce and reskill the old to 'hit the ground running' when the economy picked up. We are hearing similar suggestions today.

Vocational education and training

Traditional academic education was accused by what Bates (1974) called the MSC's *New Vocationalism* of failing to respond to a changing economy. The MSC claimed to provide young people with a new and liberating kind of learning based on what people could do rather than what they could write about in academic exams. As a result, Britain became, 'the first country to introduce competence-based assessment as the sole and mandatory approach for a large section of its education and training system' (Wolf 1994: 3). Eventually this found its way into classrooms through the Technical Vocational and Education Initiative (TVEI) in schools and colleges. TVEI was originally intended by Thatcher's Education Minister, Sir Keith Joseph, to reintroduce a 'technical' stream within comprehensive schools since he thought selection between schools no longer possible. TVEI did not turn out as Joseph intended (Jones 1989, Dale 1990) basically because school teachers and college lecturers used the extra money available to develop new and imaginative activities with their students (Ainley 1990). It was eventually curtailed following the imposition on all state schools of the academic National Curriculum in 1988.

The reality of youth training under the Tories was that it became no more than a way of managing but also disguising youth unemployment. The Youth Opportunities Programme and the even more unpopular YTS that followed, did not lead to new employment opportunities. Neither did they win the support of young people who simply didn't believe the claims of government ministers and their increasingly expensive advertising campaigns. Consequently, even if they sought the ideological high ground by portraying young people as deficient and dependent, MSC schemes experienced a crisis of legitimacy, especially when they became compulsory. There was even a national school students' strike against compulsion in 1985. The 'training allowance' was well below current youth wage rates and with inflation rising, its real value fell further. This put pressure on wages as a whole as trainees who were working with real employers (as opposed to agency and college-run make-work schemes) and nearing the end of their one and then two-year 'traineeship' could be 'substituted' by new cohorts of subsidised school leavers – just as had happened in the 1930s (Greenwood 1933).

As a result, young people voted with their feet. As the social security system became more difficult to access for anybody below the age of 18, school retention rates rose, especially following the introduction in 1986 of unitary GCSEs in place of selection for academic O-levels or CSEs. The broken promises associated with 'youth training' have continued. To this day, few young people consider the array of opportunities for 'work placements' for school and college leavers or 'internships' for graduates will ever lead to real jobs.

This period that began with the repudiation by Old Labour of their previous comprehensive policy in favour of vocational training was described by Dan Finn in 1987 as representing *Training Without Jobs*. It was essentially a hybrid and transitional phase – preceding a much greater and more prolonged intrusion of education into the lives of young people signalled by the 1988 Education Act together with the 1992 Further and Higher Education Act. These two Acts marked the end of the half-hearted and under-funded effort at constructing a German 'dual-system'. This separated initial academic education for a minority (with cuts to HE in the 1980s) from vocational training represented by YTS for the majority. In its place, a US system of general education for all was introduced as the foundation for 'lifelong learning' with tests and examinations in the academic National Curriculum as a means of competition between schools and colleges. As in the USA, 'drop-outs', stigmatised by New Labour as NEETs = Not in Education Employment or Training (originally 'Status Zero'), were to become the subject of recurrent concern.

As Jones and Wallace wrote in 1992, 'Employment, training and education policies, backed by social security policies, had moved towards constructing just two groups of young people: trainees or students' (149). The new phase of policy now attempted to reverse the proportions of these two groups from a majority of trainees and a minority of students in the 1980s towards a majority of students (at least to age 18) and a minority of trainees in the 1990s. Moreover, in contrast to the succession of discredited Youth Training Schemes, young people (and adults) did not have to be dragooned into further and higher education. In many cases they were prepared to enrol enthusiastically, despite the mounting personal indebtedness this entailed for them in the case of HE as maintenance grants were frozen, loans and then fees introduced in the 1990s.

Faced with declining employment opportunities and the failure of *Training Without Jobs*, young working-class people, qualified and encouraged by improved overall results in unitary GCSEs, increasingly decided to remain full-time in 'new school sixth forms' or go to college. They were also urged to do so by the new importance that politicians assigned to education. Following Thatcher's opening of the national economy to deregulate, or rather reregulate, global competition after the 'Big Bang' in the City of London in 1986, economic policy was abandoned to 'the free market' and officially made subservient to education. This was signalled by the dissolution of the Department of Employment and its MSC into the renamed Education Department.

ERA – 'Nationalising' the school curriculum

The Education Reform Act of 1988 signalled a major turning point in the direction of education policy by introducing a ten subject traditional academic curriculum – a grammar school education for all! For the first time also, parents as consumers of education services received written information about the requirements of its various 'key stages'. More controversially, children were subjected to end of stage Standard Assessment Tests. These measured not only their individual performance but also the performance of their schools which, in the name of 'accountability', were ranked in league tables for ease of 'parental choice' – although, as it soon became clear, schools were choosing parents, rather than the other way round. The nationalisation of the curriculum was strongly opposed by teacher unions and by 'free market' libertarian sections of the Tory Party (eg. the enobled Lord Joseph); while progressive reformers were alarmed at the academic and 'ethnocentric' bias of the National Curriculum and the pruning of non-traditional subjects such as social studies.

Though the tests were opposed on ideological grounds by the largest teacher union, the National Union of Teachers (NUT), the fact that the new curriculum soon became a bureaucratic nightmare added to the support amongst teachers for a successful boycott of SATs in 1993. This led to the first of many 'reviews' of the National Curriculum. So began a process of streamlining, particularly at Key Stage 4 (14–16 year olds) as the government announced its intention of offering 'vocational alternatives' for disaffected students. These proposals represented a step back from the inclusive idea of a National Curriculum and a return to the pre-comprehensive notions of the 1944 Act. Since then the National Curriculum has been repeatedly overloaded with worthy cross-curricular themes and at the same time dismantled in favour of personalised differentiation.

The idea of a National Curriculum needs to be separated from discussion of its content. Jones (1989) links the origins of the Conservative National Curriculum with 'New Right' emphasis on the importance of schools in transmitting traditional cultural values. The National Curriculum requirements officially replaced child-centredness by subject-centredness as even infant schools were to meet 'the needs of the economy' as defined by employers. Ironically however, as progressive approaches were squeezed out by reversion to traditional subject disciplines in schools and sixth forms, and while vocational alternatives mainly in FE were still seen as second best, performance levels in mainstream public examinations continued to rise. In fact, there was what Alison Wolf (2002) called 'a bandwagon effect' as more and more young people signed up for the academic subjects that were seen as the only route to the ever-receding goal of secure employment.

This signalled the predominance of what Phil Cohen (1997: 229) called 'the career code' over the traditional 'apprenticeship code' in structuring the social reproduction of 'a working class without work'. It accompanied the dissolution of the oppositional working-class culture of Old Labourism based upon the trades unions. Its associated conceptions of skill were largely lost in what became life-long learning in place of lifelong earning – for men at least. For young women, the National Curriculum had the unforeseen effect of boosting their exam performance in all the subjects that were now compulsory. They embraced 'the career code' as new possibilities opened up for them in the service sector using new technology. Only a minority of girls, including persisting groups of young mothers, were left behind as previous concern for 'girls' underachievement' in school switched to boys.

Together with the 1992 Further and Higher Education Act, the ERA also marked the extension of the contracting principle of the new market state to the whole of education and training. Control of state education was steadily removed from democratically accountable local authorities to be vested in central government funding agencies. Schools, colleges and previously self-governing universities bid against each other and private providers in competition to meet national targets. The quality of this delivery was inspected by centralised auditing agencies. Increasingly blurring the boundaries between private and state provision, this is a new mixed economy (as opposed to the old welfare state mixed economy in which there were generally clear divisions between state and private sectors). In this new mixed economy, a semi-privatised state sector is indiscriminately mixed with a state-subsidised private sector. It moves towards the dominance of the latter over every aspect of social life (see Whitfield 2001).

Local Management of Schools (LMS) gave schools almost complete autonomy over their budgets including staffing. Grant Maintained Status (GMS) allowed them to 'opt-out' of Local Education Authority (LEA) borough or county council control completely. Again, this was supposed to 'free' them from local bureaucratic control but the Conservative education project was the most centralised and state-centred ever. Typically, it offered more choice but less freedom. It was only off-set by concessions to devolution in the national regions of Scotland, Wales and Northern Ireland. In England, the post-1944 national system of education locally administered became the post-1988 national system nationally administered (Ainley 2001). As teacher trade unions lamented the disappearance of their members' professional autonomy over what they taught, the ten-subject National Curriculum was imposed on all English school students (except those in the private sector of course). If the National Curriculum had afforded an 'entitlement' for all students, which is how it was sold to teachers, for New Labour government it took on a 'modernising' role conflated with competition.

New Labour and 'the knowledge economy'

Tony Blair placed 'education, education, education' at the heart of government. Typically seeking to reconcile irreconcilables, New Labour sought to adapt society to what it saw as the essentially benign effects of globalisation. Building on many of the Tories' ideas, they also placed education in a new 'global' context. For young people, New Labour attempted to secure a new 'settlement', going much further than the limitations of the 1944 settlement to create a 'mass' further and higher, if not 'lifelong', education system.

Like the Tories, New Labour emphasised concern with standards – though it also modified some of the more right-wing and 'Conservative' aspects of the National Curriculum. The anachronistic Section 28 that had forbidden 'encouraging homosexuality' by teaching about it (!) was repealed and new courses like 'citizenship' introduced. New Labour, however, was more concerned with increasing the general level of performance, although raising standards for the majority did not imply that it challenged the privileges of the few.

Throughout the post-war period, governments had emphasised the importance of education as 'human capital' but now the new globalised economies provided, it was argued, unlimited opportunities for those with 'skills' – or, at least, qualifications as proxies for 'skills'. New Labour went much further. Rather than education policy supporting more general economic policy, for Blair education was the best economic policy as the survival of UK plc depended on the flexibility of its labour force. Education was no longer seen as skilling the young and reskilling the old to keep up with the latest computerised technology but was envisioned as actually generating employment through enterprising activities in a new 'knowledge economy'. *Living on thin air*, as one of Blair's advisers put it (Leadbeater 1999), like the short-lived dot.com bubble. 'Knowledge', it was alleged, had taken over as the key factor of production from more traditional economic variables such as wages and raw materials – even industrial premises and equipment. So all that was needed for 'knowledge-based economies' to flourish in global competition was adequate supplies of highly educated 'knowledge-based' workers. Thus, the discourse lost any connection with reality.

Nevertheless, central to much of the discussion about the implications of globalisation was the recognition that individual nation states had lost their ability to even regulate economic activity as multinational firms uprooted themselves from their national bases and the flow of financial capital became intercontinental. As far as economics was concerned, this meant that post-war Keynesian 'demand' side management had to give way to a concentration on the 'supply' side. Hence the Blairite obsession with elevating education to the top table of politics with its supply of so-called 'skills' certified by qualifications. People only had themselves to blame if they did not take advantage of this offer by 'an enabling state' to upskill themselves and end their 'dependency' by becoming 'fully employable'. 'Full employability' in the new market state was therefore very different from full employment in the old welfare state. Aside from reducing social security provision, there were other reasons why Britain as a 'learning society' had to learn its way to a 'knowledge economy'. Early in his premiership Blair emphasised that the country would 'succeed or fail on the basis of how it changes itself and gears up to the new economy based on knowledge' (quoted in Ball 2008: 12).

As Jones (2003) recognises, ideas about globalisation and the knowledge economy were much more amenable to New Labour than to previous Conservative administrations still shackled with nationalist and Europhobic tendencies. Blair and New Labour wanted Britain to be the country happiest to endorse globalisation and also to promote London as the most cosmopolitan and international of all cities. As a result, they made full use of the Tories' deregulation policies to ensure the 'City' – now moved down river to Canary Wharf – became a global financial hub, while employment in manufacturing, which was associated with the 'old' economy rather than the new, continued to decline with further deskilling and outsourcing to developing economies like China.

New Labour's project was social as well as economic. In his first speech as Premier on education at the University of Greenwich (on 1 November 2007), Gordon Brown continued to endorse the potential of economic globalisation as emphatically as Blair, emphasising the 'unlimited global desire for more talent'. Compared with post-war society, Brown claimed that in the twentyfirst century there is 'more room at the top'. In other words, gaining educational qualifications creates the potential for significant amounts of what sociologists term 'absolute social mobility' – everyone can move up!

Making the case for *Staying in Education and Training post-16*, the 2007 Green Paper *Raising Expectations* emphasised that there would be few openings for those without high levels of qualifications as the occupational structure was said to be changing dramatically with a 25 per cent decline in low-skilled occupations between 1984 and 2004. Therefore, 'It is no longer a sensible option for a young person to leave education for good at age 16' (DfES 2007a: 5). Even as boom turned to bust, Brown's statements showed no let up as he maintained that 'however tough the months ahead will be, it is likely in the next two decades the world economy will double in size. As many as one billion new jobs for skilled workers will be created' (Foreword to White Paper *New Opportunities: Fair Chances for the Future*, January 2009).

'Excellence for Everyone'

The 1997 White Paper *Excellence in Schools* detailed New Labour's plans to raise performance levels and 'standards' to boost 'the knowledge economy'. Though a deluge of often overtly more controversial policy statements have followed, this document remains the one in which the New Labour project for education and for young people was most clearly laid out. In place of Tory elitism, Labour promised to raise attainment of the many, rather than the few.

Excellence accordingly began with primary schools. Baseline assessments would be carried out on entry to an early start at nursery and 80 per cent of 11 year olds would be expected to reach the standards expected for their age by 2002 – 75 per cent in maths. This would not be achieved by using the discredited child-centred and activity based 'Plowden' approaches of the 1970s. Teachers clinging to this orthodoxy had produced a situation where 'too many children have poor literacy and numeracy skills' (2.20). Consequently, 'at least an hour' of literacy and numeracy instruction would now take place for all primary students everyday (2.37).

Excellence went on to set out New Labour's more general intentions. All state schools would have challenging targets. They would be provided with a wealth of comparative data to help identify differences between particular groups of students and help gauge progress against other schools in the area. Performance data (the Tories' league tables) would also continue to be published and Ofsted inspections would be central with Chris Woodhead, the Tories' favourite 'scourge of the teachers' still in charge – at least for a while. A 'Standards Task Force' reporting directly to the Secretary of State would be established to lead the crusade. All schools would be expected to succeed and there would be 'zero tolerance' of those that failed. A variety of initiatives were established to 'support' schools failing to reach the set standards in public examinations. In the most recent, secondary schools achieving less than 30 per cent A-C at GCSE have become part of a 'National Challenge', threatened with being closed or turned into state-funded but privately sponsored Academies.

If the Tories saw democratically responsive Local Education Authorities as symptomatic of what was wrong with education, then New Labour went about changing their role. Rather than being local monopoly providers of education, LEAs (now Local Authorities) were transformed into local regulators of children's services. In particular, they have played a policing role – helping to ensure that schools meet national targets and if they don't, deciding what action to take against them. So, LAs were instructed to prepare local 'Development Plans', which set out programmes of school improvement.

While adapting the previous government's conception of 'excellence', New Labour accepted many of the ideas that made up the Tories' internal market. They maintained Local Management of Schools (LMS) and – rather than abolishing them – turned Grant Maintained Schools into Foundation Schools, nominally part of the Local Authority but continuing to enjoy much greater autonomy. The 2001 Education Act extended the principle of 'choice and diversity' to the secondary sector. For some Labour supporters, this was a deadweight on the effort to raise standards (eg. Melissa Benn and Fiona Millar's 2006 *A Comprehensive Future*). Overriding its internal critics, the government forged ahead with its plans, not only to turn every school into a 'specialist' school concentrating on a particular curriculum area but, more controversially, to set up more Academies. Initially designed to replace 'failing schools' in inner city/urban areas, it soon became clear that Academies could be established anywhere and that all new secondary schools would have to have Academy status.

Government also claimed to be offering young people more choices specific to their 'needs' through a more 'personalised' and flexible curriculum. Returning to ideas in the Conservative-sponsored Dearing reports, it continued to promote specialist 'pathways' at post-14. It shelved the proposals from the Tomlinson working group to integrate (however mildly) academic and vocational learning into a common framework including A-levels. Instead, the 2005 White Paper on 14-19 education announced a programme of 14 specialist 'vocational' diplomas. Again this separated young people into two types – the academic and the vocational, though (again) with the same supposed 'parity of esteem' between them as had figured in the 1944 Education Act.

Piloting would start from September 2008 but all Key Stage 4 students would be 'entitled' to take a diploma by 2013. Much of the justification for the diplomas remained economic. The White Paper reiterated the challenges that globalisation presented and announced that the diplomas would be developed by Sector Skills Councils thus placing 'employers in the driving seat' (as in FE and increasingly in HE). The 14-19 White Paper also returned to the issue of literacy and numeracy and to perennial employer concerns about low standards. It announced a new 'functional skills' programme in English, maths and Information and Communication Technologies (ICT). Not only would these 'functional' (previously 'core', 'key' or 'basic') 'skills' be integral to the diplomas but from 2010 they would also be mandatory in GCSE English, maths and ICT – since dropped! This requirement would predictably – and perhaps intentionally – drive many young people away from the diplomas.

The most important feature of New Labour's education project however, particularly in relation to its policies for the school sector, is that it has remained highly centralised – run like an *Education PLC* (Ball, 2007 following Green and Ainley 1996). While internal marketisation has been significant in terms of the provision of education, the extent of privatisation of the school system, though important, was limited. Competition between schools also continued to play a significant role but the main emphasis has been on achieving national performance targets, supported by a series of 'national strategies'. As noted above, these were initially geared to improving literacy and numeracy but were soon extended across the primary and secondary curriculum as a whole. The idea was that 'raising standards' would enable half of young people to reach the 5 A*-C GCSE threshold for progression via Level 3 to some sort of higher education. Early years' education was not exempt with nursery education increasingly referred to as 'Foundation Stage' with its own standards and targets.

Consistently, New Labour identified with and gave a prime role to the ideas of the 'school improvement' movement. This had been taken up by educational researchers from the London University Institute of Education. They claimed to discover blueprints – particular types of management structure, leadership and communication styles – that could be used everywhere to the same effect. School improvers were therefore disparaging towards attempts to 'excuse' educational underperformance in terms of social factors such as class, race and gender. Success or failure is, they argued, the product of the 'internal' features of the school or college. Such improvement techniques have obvious links with a business model, rather than an educational one. They have contributed to the 'data revolution' in schools, colleges and subsequently universities, where everything is tracked and recorded and improved outputs are seen as the product of more effective inputs.

New Labour's business plan for teachers

Since the post-war years and beyond, even if their levels of pay hardly reflected those in other 'professional' occupations and were often well below those enjoyed by their mainland European counterparts, school teachers – like F&HE lecturers – benefited from secure employment. They also enjoyed extensive 'professional autonomy' over what they taught in the classroom and how learning took place. This was seen as the culmination of a long journey to achieve professional status with graduate-entry through Schools of Education attached to HE in place of the former FE 'trade' teacher training colleges (Roy 1968). As a result, in many schools styles of teaching continued to be rather old fashioned with drilling in pre-Plowden primaries and many secondary moderns while grammar teachers stood in front of the class 'transmitting' the intricacies of their particular academic subjects. 'Professional autonomy' allowed a diversity of practices – including those considered progressive and radical and referred to above.

As part of the campaign to 'raise standards' this teacher culture had to be 'remodelled' with New Labour claiming that it exhibited a Luddite mentality (Allen 1999). If the whole education system was to be run on business lines, occupational security (lost to HE under the 1992 Further and Higher Education Act and in FE previously following a long dispute) would have to be seriously curtailed. So would the influence of teachers and lecturers over the direction of learning. Teachers and lecturers were the frontline troops for raising standards but whilst being 'operationally central', were 'strategically marginal' (Jones 2003: 162).

Weakening the 'professional autonomy' of individual teachers remained key to New Labour's education policies. Teachers as a profession and the organisations that represent them, such as the National Union of Teachers – considered a 'professional partner' until the late 1970s – were excluded from debates about pedagogy and curriculum. Instead, these were handed over to centrally-funded programmes bid for by university researchers, if not to ubiquitous consultants. Teaching was considered a technical, rather than a creative or intellectual activity and practitioners were expected to comply with national guidelines for 'lesson delivery' and be seen to adopt strategies supposed to maximise 'learning outputs'.

Today, failure to comply means risking being considered 'unsatisfactory' on a rigidly imposed Ofsted lesson grading scale. To ensure that as much of the learning process is quantified as possible, as with the literacy and numeracy strategies referred to above, there has been an emphasis on teaching discrete competences or items of information in a tightly constrained way. Rather than encouraging students to read entire books for example, teachers concentrate on extracts. These teaching methods are inculcated during post-graduate training that, although it has moved into what is now higher education, is actually competence-based training in standards dictated by a central government agency and so an example of FE in HE (as opposed to HE in FE).

The 'personalisation' of learning for pupils has also taken on a rather different connotation compared with previously when it might have been associated with encouraging children to pursue individual project work integrating inquiry across an array of subjects. Under New Labour, teachers were provided with tons of data about the performance of each individual pupil and expected to use this to monitor progress and predict future 'outcomes'. As in the Health Service, where personal care packages can be individually costed, this prepared the ground for a free basic package – paid with a voucher perhaps – topped up by payments for 'extras' for those who can afford them. 'Guaranteed entitlements,' as Lord Mandelson told BBC Radio 4's *Today* programme (15 September 2009), 'are the new frontier of public sector reform'.

A performance management culture also means that a teacher's failure to meet targets for particular pupils may result in not moving up the salary scale. If irregularities persist, 'competency' charges can be invoked and disciplinary action for dismissal after failure in 'a teaching MOT'. This followed a 1998 Green Paper which had picked up on the Tory Education Minister, Ken Clarke's idea of performance-related pay but which was ruled unlawful by the High Court in July 2000.

To reinforce this new style 'professionalism', New Labour also established a General Teaching Council (GTC) and equivalent Higher Education Academy. (They didn't bother with an FE one, although they did talk about it for a while.) While over half of GTC members are drawn from the teaching profession and most of these are either elected or represent teacher trade unions, the Council has also been designed as yet another forum through which government ideas about teaching can be relayed to teachers. A national programme of 'Continuing Professional Development' ensures that in-service professional development also reflects national aims and priorities.

In the past, teaching to all levels was relatively collegial and non-hierarchical with pay differences reflecting 'seniority' or administrative workloads that lecturers in F&HE often took in turn. Now schools, colleges and universities have become more hierarchical with management structures reflecting those of the private sector. 'School improvement' has created a new 'leadership culture'. A National College of School Leadership has been established to create a 'leadership cadre', not only responsible for raising standards but also for promoting the sorts of practices that allow this to happen. With headteachers and principals providing 'strategic leadership' in the role of Chief Executives – particularly in larger schools or groups of schools and in colleges – it is debated whether they need to have ever been teachers themselves. At present the vast majority of heads continue to have classroom experience but Senior Leadership Teams regularly comprise non-teaching personnel with accountancy or business experience (*TES Magazine*, 6 March 2009). This is also seen as important in the governance of HE with even the University of Cambridge capitulating to government demands for businesspersons on its Court of Governors. If excluded from 'strategic decisions', armies of 'middle managers' and still more 'consultants' have also emerged charged with promoting good practice. They also 'monitor' their colleagues by regularly observing their lessons and recording and analysing their performances.

Meanwhile, classroom teachers are surrounded by what the architect of many of New Labour policies, Michael Barber (1996), described as 'para-professionals' – not only classroom assistants but 'cover supervisors'. Their use threw teacher unions like the National Union of Teachers (NUT) into disarray, rightly identifying them as a way of deskilling the profession but recognising that its members identify 'cover' as one of the most stressful and inconvenient tasks they have to undertake. These developments have been part of a more general 'remodelling of the schools workforce' introduced by successive governments to allow teachers more time to 'concentrate on teaching', ie. to raise standards, rather than pursue clerical and administrative tasks. As well as cover supervisors, the increased use of teaching assistants and the possibility that they can be used at the expense of teachers, has been facilitated by the way in which the curriculum has been packaged to clarify content and rigidify assessment objectives.

As part of its drive to replace a 'producer dominated' culture in schools, New Labour sought to reduce the professional autonomy of teachers in other ways. For example, the balance of forces between teachers and their students has changed as schools have been required to 'consult children' (again, as in the previous Student Satisfaction Survey piloted in FE and then extended to HE). Schools are not only asked to consider greater pupil involvement through school councils and by appointing pupils as associate governors, they are asked to involve them in teaching staff appointments and – most controversially – as 'consumers' in lesson observations of their teachers following Ofsted criteria.

Schools have also transformed their relationship with parents. While largely excluded from the day-to-day running of schools, in many ways parents have been recast as customers of schools which produce 'products' = children with qualifications. Ofsted continues to see parents as one of its main constituencies, even putting off 'no notice' inspections of schools to give parents a chance to ask prior questions about their children's school and its teachers.

Further and higher education

According to the contracting principle of the new market state, the Tories nationalised Further Education Colleges by removing them from LEA control in 1993. Since then it is in what has become the Learning and Skills Sector that marketisation if not outright privatisation has gone furthest. The new corporations running the colleges were given charitable status and although still dependent on public funds were allowed to enter into commercial contracts to buy and sell services, appoint Chief Executives and adopt a business-style managerial culture aimed at maximising student numbers. In the first five years following incorporation under their own centralised funding councils from which colleges contracted to deliver 'units of resource' (= students) assessed at five different points in the year, the number of colleges fell from 465 to 373 by 2008 with the loss of more than 20,000 staff, while numbers of students and trainees spiralled to over four million today but on a reduced unit of resource (Burchill 1998). Although, in the latest in a series of reorganisations, funding for FE colleges is to be returned to Local Authorities on a formula basis, the content of their courses is dictated by the employer-run Sector Skills Councils and courses are delivered by colleges in competition with private providers.

Once providing a variety of options and offering second chances to those failed by academic schooling, the brief of FE colleges has increasingly focused on improving vocational skills. The 2006 Leitch review argued that Britain, although having more university graduates, had fallen behind its international competitors in the promotion of 'intermediate skills'. As a result adult education, unless it is directly vocational, has given way to 'Train 2 gain' where colleges bid for contracts to work directly with employers.

In higher education, the polytechnics and HE colleges, already under their own Funding Council control, were in 1992 given 'university' status. This ended the 'binary line' in HE and doubled the number of university students at a stroke. With funding also tied to student numbers, these 'new universities' were encouraged to pack in as many students as possible to compensate for the research funding enjoyed by their traditional counterparts. Mass universities for the many were thus combined with the existing elite universities for the few. In between were an uneasy group of campus universities anxious not to fall below the new binary line dividing the mainly-teaching from the also-researching that would predictably be redrawn higher up the system. The freezing of maintenance grants and the introduction of student loans in the early 1990s also paved the way for the introduction of tuition fees by New Labour in 1997.

The New Labour government accepted the widely anticipated and bipartisan recommendation of the 1997 Dearing Report on Higher Education to introduce annual undergraduate student fees of £1,000 a year rising with inflation. Ending free public higher education in England, fees fitted the government's model of education as an investment in an individual's human capital for the future rather than as an entitlement. Breaking a 2005 Manifesto commitment, fees were raised again to a new 'cap' of £3000 in 2006. Further rises, most probably uncapped to follow the free market in post-graduate and overseas student fees and differentiated by subject and institution, can be anticipated following a repeatedly postponed review. After all, with students queuing to get into HE, it only made sense from a business point of view to charge more. 'Invest now, cash in later', is the message transmitted to the thousands of new students who enter the university sector today.

Delayed transition

The widening participation by more young people in some form of further and higher education has not meant that the lifestyles of the predominantly middleclass students of the 1960s, '70s and '80s have been adopted by all of them. For a start, this is no longer a minority experience – government claims 80 per cent remaining in school or college at 16 and aims at 50 per cent of 18–30 year olds to have 'some experience of higher education' by 2010 (43.3 per cent in 2007/08 = 47 per cent of all girls but only 42 per cent of boys, reversing the previous male preponderance). In addition, the abolition of grants and the introduction of loans and fees has created 'a new type of student' (Allen 2004). Rather than 'going away' to a campus life in another part of the country, often interrupted by the now customary 'gap year,' the new generation of students are as likely to remain at home.

This is particularly the case in large urban areas where there are several HE institutions within commuting distance. Living at home whilst studying reduces the intensity of traditionally compressed 3 year subject degree courses. So does part-time HE and combined degrees which are likely to become popular as students 'spread their bets' for 'flexibility'. Indeed, 'the student experience is a part-time one for most students' (Brennan et al. 2009: 12), not only because terms are so short but because one in three undergraduates are part time (ibid.). Especially for students who remain at home to study, their experience is that going to university is something to be fitted into existing lifestyles rather than marking a transition to new ones (see Chapter 4). They emphasise the similarities of 'going to uni' rather than the differences with their post-16 experiences. Differences are only relative: improved access to library resources and better IT facilities but less contact with teachers, for instance (Allen 2004). 'Going to uni' is often only an extension of attending similar courses in sixth form or at FE college; indeed, one in ten undergraduates take their HE in FE (HEFCE 2009) – not counting Foundation 'degrees' and the Higher National Diplomas they replace (see next chapter).

Compared with the 1960s when the link between leaving school, leaving home and getting married was at its most compressed for working-class youngsters, by the end of the twentieth century, relationships between young people and their parents/ carers have changed significantly. Prolonging education, including attending university, has meant prolonging dependency, either on parents or the state and loans. It has created a new form of 'semi-dependency' and an 'extended transition', formerly only regularised for middleclass youth via university residence. Nowadays, even for those following this established pattern, 'transition' is incomplete if they return home after graduation or postgraduation.

This alters the post-war 'settlement' between the welfare state and young people. In this chapter we have used this term to describe particular arrangements between young people and society reflected in the part played by education and training in their lives. The current period of extended education for 'employability' has significantly increased the importance of education for almost all young people. This has replaced the classic post-war 'apprentice boy' model of leaving school, starting work and getting married in quick succession before lifelong earning often in one craft trade or 'job for life' (from 15–65 for most men at least). Even for the largely middleclass minority then in HE, their undergraduate degree was usually 'final'.

'Education for employability' has filled the vacuum left by the decline in 'youth jobs' and traditional industrial apprenticeships. As noted earlier, in the mid-1960s, a quarter of a million young people were entering apprenticeships annually and, with almost a third of young people as a whole finding work in manufacturing, unemployment amongst youth remained lower than for the population as a whole. Even if employment opportunities in the manufacturing sector have crumbled and the time-served apprenticeship has all but vanished, it might have been expected that the four million-plus service sector jobs created between 1970 and the end of the twentieth century would have provided new employment openings for young people. But much of this work is only part-time and deskilled so that, as Mizen points out (56), many employers have continued to prefer more 'stable' or 'mature' employees, such as married women returning to work on 'twilight' shifts. Thus unemployment amongst young people since the 1980s has remained largely what economists refer to as 'structural'.

This situation was accentuated by 'cyclical' factors – repeated periods of economic stagnation with slack labour markets. In 1986 almost one in four 18 to 19 year olds were unemployed. It is only since then and especially in the period of expansion at the end of the 1990s, that service sector employers have been more reliant on youth. Yet, as chapter three describes, in the current downturn youth unemployment has climbed again. As a result, learning rather than earning has become the new norm for many young people, despite often combining 'full-time' education with 'part-time' employment (often full-time as well if it is available).

The chapters that follow will show how New Labour's education project sought to create a new prolonged learning settlement between young people and the state. Unlike the stop-gap Youth Training programmes that preceded it, which, as we noted, young people rejected by 'voting with their feet' to remain at school or go to college, staying on in education has been achieved largely 'voluntarily' with many HE students taking out loans to afford it. It was only with the Education and Skills Bill published in November 2007 that New Labour legislated to raise the minimum age of participation in education or training. This was a consequence of concern about the 'underclass' of NEETS, officially estimated at just under 10 per cent of 16–18s in 2007. It is unlikely that this ROSLA2 (raising the school leaving age to 17 in 2013 and 18 by 2015) which gives young people the option of full-time education, part-time training while working or an apprenticeship, will be able to prevent hard core NEETs slipping through the net. With youth unemployment reaching alarming proportions, the concept of NEET itself may well have to be redefined. While Jones (2009: 99) is right to say that the welfare state age-related settlement has become 'destandardised', the two socially acceptable types of young people that the government aims to create post-18 are now students or apprentices – both without jobs.

More than a decade after arriving in office, public support for Labour's education policies declined to an all-time low. The next chapter will examine the contradictions and limitations of the 'standards agenda' to account for why this occurred, while Chapter 3 will revisit and question New Labour's claims about education and economic prosperity in the context of an increasingly polarised jobs market, stunted social mobility and the most severe economic downturn since the 1920s.

2

Overtested and Undereducated

Making good progress or running out of steam?

This chapter examines the deadening routine that New Labour's standards agenda has imposed upon the rising generation for whom 'quality' has only been achieved at mounting cost. An on-going crisis over National Curriculum Assessment and the SATs tests was combined with problems implementing new initiatives, such as the 14-19 diplomas. The chapter asks whether these government attempts to promote a new learning culture in schools really met with the success they claimed. This is the most academically certified generation ever – 'tested to destruction', as has been said – yet there are widespread allegations that meeting targets and 'teaching to test' are being given preference at the expense of really improving literacy and numeracy suggesting that today's youngsters are overtested but undereducated.

More pupils are taking and more are passing exams than ever before. If judged in terms of the criteria used by government, then in many respects the 'standards' agenda has been a success. Pass rates in public examinations now stand at levels that would have been considered inconceivable 30 years ago. The numbers gaining 5 A*-C GCSE, a benchmark with which the government became almost obsessed, reached 65.7 per cent in 2008 – the largest increase since 1990 and a 20 per cent increase since 1997 when New Labour came into office. In total, almost 100,000 more students gained 5 A*-C GCSEs than in 1997. Only

3 per cent gained no grades at all – down from 7 per cent in 1997. In addition, 2008 produced the largest annual rise in the number of students getting the top grades since 1989, with 20.7 per cent reaching A or A* – an increase of 1.2 per cent on the previous year. In 2009, GCSE grades reached another record level with 67.1 per cent of entries receiving A*-C and more than 1 in 5 exam entries being awarded A or A*. There was also an increase in the number of students opting for more traditional subjects, with entries for maths, biology, chemistry and physics all rising – more students than ever also took their GCSE maths papers a year earlier.

As has been the case in recent years, girls continued to outperform boys in the top grades with 8.2 per cent of all their scripts being awarded A* for GCSE, compared with 6.0 per cent for boys and 26.9 per cent of girls achieving an A grade at A-level compared with the 24.6 per cent of boys – with the same gender gaps even in supposedly 'boy-friendly' science subjects and technology. Single sex girls' schools continued to top league tables in both the state and private sector.

The DfES 2007 consultation document *Making good progress* trumpeted government success in promoting 'excellence for everyone'. It pointed out that the number of 'all ability schools' where 70 per cent or more of students gain 5 A*-C GCSEs rose six-fold between 1997 and 2006 to more than 500. The document also recorded that the number of schools where only a quarter of students obtain 5 A*-Cs has fallen from 600 in 1997 to just 62. In 2009, 280 schools, a fall from 440 the previous year, failed to reach the government's latest benchmark of a minimum of 30 per cent students gaining the 5 A*-C.

The increases in performance for A-level are no less impressive, especially when it is recalled that it was a qualification designed for and taken by only 5 per cent of 18 year olds when it replaced the former matriculation certificate in 1951. In 2009 there were a record 846,977 entries, 1.17 million for the intermediate AS levels. Pass rates reached 97.5 per cent, up from 97.2 per cent the previous year. A grades went to 26.7 per cent of all entries, up from 25.9 per cent in 2008. Oxford University was expected to turn away 12,000 students with three straight As and from 2010 candidates will probably be required to have the new A* grade. (*Independent* 13 August 2009).

Degree pass rates have also risen relentlessly with many graduates achieving the once rare first class and half obtaining upper seconds. Few except Vice Chancellors – unable to explain to the 2009 House of Commons Select Committee on Universities why this had occurred but implying that it was too complicated for mere mortals to understand – accept that this reflects any increase in standards on mainly unchanged academic programmes. In fact, reading between the lines of JMConsulting's 2008 report to the Higher Education Funding Council for England on *The Sustainability of Learning and Teaching in English Higher Education*, it is clear that something will have to be done soon to sustain standards of even basic undergraduate literacy, while in many subjects foundation courses in the maths required have had to be introduced.

Driving up standards or dumbing them down?

The increase in pass rates in public examinations, particularly at A-level has led to accusations of 'dumbing down' – especially from those sections of education for whom A-level was once a 'gold standard', a way of protecting their exclusivity. In 2003 allegations that exam boards were tampering with grade boundaries as a result of pressure from government, led to the resignation of the Qualification and Curriculum Authority's Chief Executive. Controversy over standards of comparability continued with the Headmaster of Eton complaining in *The Times* (20 November 2006) that A-levels now only teach students to 'think inside a very small box' and that they discriminate against 'highly imaginative students', whose answers are often marked down because they are considered too sophisticated.

It is not merely an issue of general standards. Knowing there are inconsistencies in grades awarded between the now-privatised exam boards, schools 'shop around' – changing from one board to another to improve their league table position on which their future recruitment and funding depends. Policing the standards agenda so as to maintain public confidence has become a nightmare. So much so that in 2007 a new regulatory body, 'Ofqual', was created. Inevitably one quango was drawn into conflict with another; in this case with the QCA, the agency still responsible for the development of what was left of the National Curriculum. In March 2009 for example, Ofqual told more than half a million students that their science GCSE pass grades last year were higher than they should have been because the papers had not been challenging enough; there were too many multi-choice questions and standards differed widely across the major examination boards. Ofqual's intervention resulted in awarding bodies having to make hasty changes to their 2009 papers.

With so many schools learning how to play the system for maximum advantage and with exam boards developing new courses as well as changing old ones to attract new customers, teachers also realise the only way they can assure success is to spend as much time teaching exam technique as they do teaching the syllabus. As outlined in Chapter 1, the new centralised 'strategies' give teachers little choice but to deliver lessons in particular ways. This type of 'teaching' has become so ingrained that many teachers have lost all notion of how it could ever be any different and a whole new generation, entering via standards-based training, have no understanding of the 'professional judgement' which was considered central to teacher autonomy up until the late 1980s.

It is impossible to prove and counterproductive to speculate about whether the latest versions of GCSE and A-levels are easier or harder than their predecessors; but there is no doubt that students and their teachers are better at preparing for them. In fact, passing examinations has become for many no more than an exercise in 'information processing'. In knowing what they have to do and when they have to do it, rather than having to 'understand', young people have adopted a pragmatic attitude; for example, never needing to read a whole book, only exerts and anthologies. In collecting the information they need, disregarding what they don't, they are aided by the growing and lucrative industry of revision guides, street-corner crammers and ubiquitous personal tutoring, all of variable price and quality. For teachers in schools and colleges, 'raising standards' is about being expert in examination procedures, up to date with examiner and moderator reports and deferring to clearly defined 'mark schemes'. For students, 'We learn more but we think less', as one 16 year old FE student told Vernell (in London Region of the University and College Union no date: 3).

The transformation of learning into information processing has also been greatly facilitated by the increased power of ICT to facilitate cutting and pasting on demand. Just as Wikipedia has replaced the encyclopaedia, a visit to any classroom will provide more than enough examples of 'researching' reduced to 'googling'. We argue in Chapter 4 that this also affects much educational research but for pupils and students it can result in a situation where, as Maryanne Wolf notes, many 'are not illiterate but they may never become true expert readers' (2008: 225). Again, this overschooling and undereducating is endemic, merely manifesting itself in different ways at various levels of learning. Instead of comprehending the situation as a whole, commentators and academics often apportion blame only to particular features of it – the modularisation of courses, for example.

Retakes and appeals

The division of undergraduate and postgraduate degrees, A-levels (and in future GCSEs) into modularised 'units' has improved accessibility for students who previously were often unsure about syllabus content, let alone what they were expected to do to obtain certain grades. It has also encouraged students to re-sit even those units they have already passed so as to achieve higher grades and improve their overall scores. So it is common in sixth forms for example, for those taking A2 units in their second year to also be retaking one, two or even three units they have already completed at AS level in their first year. Indeed, with AS contributing 50 per cent of the total mark but being considerably less difficult than A2, it would make no sense to do otherwise.

Public doubts about the current examination system can only be confirmed by recent reports of more than 60,000 candidates given the wrong grade in A-levels and GCSEs and by the revelation that in 2008 schools made over 350,000 appeals (*The Times*

19 March 2009). Grades awarded by examination boards were once considered to be sacrosanct because most boards originated from prestigious universities. When only a minority of young people went on to higher education, their workings were of little concern. The 'standards agenda' in which league tables attempt to make schools 'accountable', not to mention the way in which performance targets and grade expectations are imposed on them from outside, has changed all that. With thousands of examiners now marking hundreds of thousands of papers, the whole system is collapsing under its own weight. This spurs efforts to virtualise the whole exercise but online marking brings its own problems, especially with multiple-choice questions.

Examining the examiners took on a new significance in the summer of 2002 when leading schools, including many in the private sector, found major inconsistencies with their students' predicted performance. Over 2,000 results were upgraded and the Tomlinson review into A-level standards, later to become the 14-19 working group, was initiated by then schools minister David Miliband. The following year there were 95,000 challenges and 18,000 grade changes (*TES* 21 January 2005). Chances of success varied from board to board with AQA candidates having a 1 in 7 chance of an upgrade as compared with OCR's 1 in 17 (*TES* 24 April 2009).

According to Ofqual, even examiners themselves believe that at least 20 per cent of grades awarded are incorrect and that this problem has been exacerbated by having so many exam boards (*TES* 15 May 2009). Meanwhile, the cost of entering students has continued to rise – from £155 million in 2002/3 to £265 million in 2007/08, up £25 million from the previous year. Opposition politicians and teachers' leaders were quick to use this as ammunition in their call for examination reform. According to the Association for School and College leaders, John Dunford, examination costs have now become the second biggest item of expenditure for schools after staffing costs (*TES* 2 May 2009) – much more than they spend on books.

A culture of plagiarism

Ofqual has also had to turn its attention to other consequences resulting from the pressures of the standards agenda, bringing in a private company that has designed software to tackle the growing issue of 'plagiarism' (*TES* 20 March 2009). According to Ofqual, more than a quarter of all examination malpractice has involved various forms of plagiarism, from failure to acknowledge sources to copying from other candidates. Any internet search engine will lead to several sites offering school, college and university students advice on 'how to cheat'. Not only are new resources and new methods of cheating constantly being made available but there are also more opportunities to purchase the services of those offering to write coursework and dissertations directly. A new online industry staffed by former students gives money-back guarantees if detected (see Baldwin 2008). According to the Association of Teachers and Lecturers (ATL), 58 per cent of sixth-form teachers thought plagiarism was rife and 33 per cent estimated that half of student work contained plagiarism (*TES* 20 March 2009).

Taking unauthorised items into exam rooms is also a common offence with 60 per cent of such cases involving mobile phones. Other unauthorised items included notes, or notes in the wrong format, study guides, materials with prohibited annotations, calculators and dictionaries where banned, and personal audio players (BBC news 26 March 2006). Coursework, once welcomed by many teachers as a better and more accurate indication of a student's ability, has, for many become the complete opposite. Government restrictions on the amount of coursework now included in the new GCSE and GCE A-level syllabuses are aimed at preventing plagiarism as much as at raising attainment. In addition, according to *The Guardian* science correspondent (22 May 2008), examiners could soon be facing a different kind of drug problem as students take brain-enhancing pills to boost their speed of writing and recall. Government advisers warned that new drugs to treat conditions as varied as Alzheimer's disease, attention deficit disorder and narcolepsy are being misused by students eager to bump up their grades.

It isn't just students who have been bending the rules. According to *The TES* (14 August 2009), in a Teacher Support Network survey more than two-thirds of teachers admitted to helping pupils 'more than they should' while QCA also confirmed an increase in 'over-aiding' pupils in SATs tests. In August 2009, for instance, three teachers at a school in Bolton were suspended over claims they helped pupils with questions in oral GCSE language exams. Ofqual advises that teachers who subvert the system risk being disciplined by the GTC. The problem is endemic to the system however, with anecdotal evidence indicating dissatisfaction amongst Oxford dons that their prized one-on-one tutorials are being subverted into cramming sessions by students anxious to seek tips on likely exam questions (Misra 2007).

Cramming and tutoring

Clearly the ability to secure a place at a 'good school' and particularly to use the private sector is closely related to income, as are exam results. Increasing numbers of parents and children also employ private tutors to give them an extra 'push'. This is almost an inevitable consequence of the high stakes and increasingly competitive testing and examination system. According to the Sutton Trust 2009 (http://www.suttontrust.com/news.asp#a059), over two-fifths (43 per cent) of young people sampled in London reported receiving private tuition in some form during their school years, an increase from 36 per cent in 2005. The proportion of pupils having private tuition has increased in five years from 18 per cent to 22 per cent nationally. The scale of paid-for tutorage in London, though, is significantly higher than in any other area. The South East region is second with 28 per cent, while Yorkshire and Humber is lowest. Clearly, schools with higher examination results invariably owe their success to factors other than their standards of teaching.

While significant amounts of money are needed to buy the services of a top-level cramming college, parents can secure the services of a university student posing as a 'tutor' and offering help in one particular subject like maths, for as little as £20 per hour. The cost of a more established tutor is generally £30-£35. At best, buying in this sort of help can have psychological benefits for both parents and children concerned about 'slipping behind' in the qualifications race. But it doesn't end at school; university students also resort to tutors and extra examination coaching if they or their parents can afford it. Some universities even provide such revision courses at extra cost!

Meanwhile, former-HMI Woodhead's company Cognita in partnership with Sunny Varkey's Dubai-based GEM group with its advisory board chaired by Sir Mike Tomlinson, wait in the wings for the introduction by a Conservative government of vouchers that will subsidise a raft of private cut-price 'crammer' schools.

Testing, testing, testing

In addition to the more general crisis in confidence over examinations and standards, specific pressure points persist. If there is one area of teaching and learning under the years of education, education, education where there has been the most controversy, then it has to be the Standard Assessment Tests at 7, 11 and 14. Brought in by the Tories these were maintained by New Labour to ensure accountability and competition between schools.

As with the results for GCSE and A-levels, major improvements have been measured by SATs at National Curriculum levels. At Key Stage 2 (age 11) in 2008 nearly 100,000 additional pupils, an increase of 16 per cent, achieved the expected Level 4 standard in English compared with 1997 and 85,000 more in maths, whereas the number reaching the highest Level 5 almost doubled. Improvements in performances for 14 year olds now appear to be reaching a plateau however. English and science scores for those 14 year olds attaining Level 5 are not improving and are still well below the 85 per cent target. Achievement rates for Key Stage 2 students are now also remaining more or less static and still below target. Even Lord Adonis, then Schools Minister and one of Tony Blair's favourite educationalists, while defending the SATs and New Labour's record in raising standards, admitted that 20 per cent of primary children still left school without basic skills in reading, writing and maths (*The Guardian* 21 August 2008).

There is sound empirical evidence that the literacy and numeracy of primary and lower secondary age group children has not improved, despite well over a decade of national external testing. Professor Robin Alexander, leader of the Cambridge University review of the primary curriculum, claimed in a preliminary report that the reading ability of most children was the same as in the 1950s but that there was now a 'yawning gap between high and low-attaining pupils – bigger than in most comparable countries'(*TES* 02 November 2007). Ofsted also reported in 2008 that 20 per cent of children still left primary school functionally illiterate.

Even if more than 55 per cent of teenagers achieved an A*-C grade in maths GCSE, more than double those who gained an O-level Grade C twenty five years ago, a study by researchers at King's College London and the University of Durham (reported in *The Guardian* 05 September 2009) found that there has not been a corresponding increase in pupils' understanding of concepts such as ratio or the operations of algebra. The study showed little evidence that mathematical attainment had kept up with improvements in exam results.

According to the Organisation for Economic Cooperation and Development (OECD), in rankings compiled by the Programme for International Assessment (Pisa), England had fallen from seventh to seventeenth in reading, and eighth to twenty-fourth in maths (reported in *The Independent* 05 December 2007). The 'official' review of the primary curriculum headed by Professor (Sir) Jim Rose re-emphasised the importance of children understanding English and communication but – though referring to SATs as 'the elephant in the room' (*Independent* 30 April 2009) – was not given a remit to discuss assessment.

The anti-SATs campaign, which had faltered somewhat since the previous boycott in 1993, was given a new lease of life by the government's decision in October 2008 to scrap the 2009 Key Stage 3 tests for 14 year olds and rely instead on teacher assessment. The National Association of Headteachers (NAHT) and the National Union of Teachers (NUT) both passed motions at their annual conferences signalling a willingness to ballot. The KS3 decision followed a fiasco over marking the 2008 tests when some schools waited an extra three months for English results. It ended in government cancelling the £156 million contract with ETS, the American company to which marking had been contracted out, and the resignation of QCA Chief Executive, Ken Boston. Not only had test results arrived late, there had also been major concerns about the standard of the marking with schools reporting major inconsistencies between grades awarded and with their own expectations of their children (*TES* 22 August 2008). The headteacher of a primary school with the highest 'value added' score told *The Guardian* (02 April 2009) that his results were over-inflated and that parents shouldn't trust SATs data. A poll of more than 1,000 parents found two-thirds believed SATs a waste of time that put their children under unnecessary stress (*TES* 12 September 2009).

For government, 'not surprisingly, as we get closer towards our goals it is getting harder to make further improvements' (*Making Good Progress*: 3) This signalled a move towards a 'test when ready' system – part of a drive towards more personalised learning with testing at every National Curriculum level, rather than just at the end of every key stage. The assistant director of the prestigious National Foundation for Educational Research, Chris Whetton, described the new proposals, which in reality replaced SATs with twice-yearly testing, as a 'disaster'. He argued that they would further narrow the curriculum, demotivate pupils and would be even less reliable than the current tests (*TES* 12 September 2008). Teachers would be expected to collect even more data about their pupils' progress and be subject to even tighter forms of performance management and accountability. Neither was there any indication that there would be an end to league tables, the source of the competition.

In the end the 'Expert Group', set up by the government in the wake of the Key Stage 3 decision, advised that because the new tests were not ready and because teacher assessment was not 'rigorous enough', there was no alternative but to continue with the primary SATs in maths and English at least for the moment – the government had already decided to abandon science. This and the legal uncertainties around a test boycott, were enough to short circuit the NAHT/NUT campaign.

Desperate diplomacy

Growing dissatisfaction with the existing National Curriculum and its assessment has been matched by a less than enthusiastic reception for government attempts to introduce alternative qualifications for the half of young people who fall at the crucial 5 A*-C GCSE hurdle. This has particularly been the case with the new 14-19 specialist diplomas.

Announced in the 2005 14-19 White Paper as a qualification appropriate for up to 40 per cent of 14–16 year olds, the diplomas failed to interest employers, schools or universities. They have also been plagued with uncertainty about whether they are 'applied' or 'vocational'. Though promoted as being one the most significant changes to the secondary curriculum and one where employers would be 'in the driving seat', the final course specifications ended up being written by consultants in a desperate bid to meet the launch date. The introduction of the diploma was another attempt at establishing a 'middle track' qualification (Allen and Ainley 2008), like the previous contradiction in terms, General Vocational Qualifications. GNVQs, although originally designed as a route into the workplace, ended up as a 'second chance' qualification as students unable to enter A-level courses used them for access to local clearing universities. Like many GNVQ students, diploma candidates will be learning about the workplace without developing the specific skills needed for the job – studying construction without ever laying a brick, learning about hairdressing but never cutting hair.

Desperate to save the qualification from being squeezed between A-levels/ GCSEs and vocational qualifications for new apprenticeships, in the spring of 2008, Ed Balls announced that diplomas would be available from 2013 in more traditional subject areas like humanities, modern languages and science. There would also be an extended version equivalent to four and a half A-levels. This move was interpreted by some commentators as a sign government was moving towards replacing A-levels with diplomas but was seen by one of the authors as 'desperate diplomacy' (Allen 2007).

While research commissioned by government reported support for the diplomas from universities (*TES*, 11 September 2009), as with the GNVQ, elite/ Russell universities remained 'cynical' about the qualifications' academic rigour. Research by Reading University found that many English teenagers either still knew nothing about the diplomas or have concluded that they are a less attractive option than A-levels and not a viable route into higher education or employment (www.reading.ac.uk/about/newsand-events/releases/PR22162.aspx).

Initially diplomas were to be rolled out over a period of time with the first five 'lines' available in September 2008 for 45,000 students. Government subsequently back-tracked so that only 20,000 places were being made available in the interests of 'quality'. With provisional estimates for embedding the diplomas put at £65 million, total investment in the new qualification was expected to have reached £295 million by March 2010. Despite schools and colleges enjoying a funding premium of £1,000 for every student enrolling and government spending £7 million on publicity and marketing (Baker 2009), there were only 12,000 registered students when the courses began. Government predictions of 40,000 diploma students for 2009/10 were also premature.

As well as being reluctant to involve themselves in yet another round of new vocational qualifications, schools in particular have doubtless been put off by the difficulties of delivering the diploma. Too complex for an individual school to manage more than one – or maybe two at the most, many young people will be expected to attend other schools. Or, more likely, travel to the FE colleges that are at the hub of local diploma partnerships for up to two days a week. While headteachers have often been only too pleased to have some of their more 'disaffected' Year 10 or 11 students relocated to college for some of the week, they are less keen on allowing large groups of students to migrate to college because they will take badly needed financial resources with them. Diploma failure would be a huge political embarrassment for government, yet at the time of writing it is hard to see any other outcome, with only a fraction of the first diploma students enrolling on Level 3 (A-level equivalent) and with a future Conservative government likely to either scrap the qualification completely, or recast it as a lower level vocational qualification linked to the workplace and apprenticeships.

Academies lumber on

As with the diploma, the even more costly Academies programme has faltered, but, unlike the diploma, there is little sign of it going off the rails with 400 of these schools set to open by 2010 and more planned. London Mayor, Boris Johnson, wants to set up a ring of 'Mayor's Academies' using money from the London Development Agency. This reflects Conservative support for Academies as – if policy briefings and press releases are to be believed – a future 'Blairite' Conservative government might withdraw its overt support for grammar schools in favour of backing Academies. Covertly rather than openly selective, Academies will mimic the grammar school tradition, becoming the elite inner-city schools desired by Blair.

Academies have remained publicly funded at often exorbitant cost – so much so that it is only recently that government prepared to cut spending on its flagship programme with sponsors told to expect a reduction in funding for each new academy school in 2010 (*Guardian* 2 September 2009). Run by private contractors under the new market state model of Public Private Partnerships *Building Schools for the Future* programme which constructs them, Academies have a variety of admission policies but also an increasingly diverse array of sponsors. As Francis Beckett (2007) has pointed out, the recent involvement of Local Authorities, elite universities – even some trade unions are now interested – reflects the unwillingness of the 'household names' of British capitalism to become involved. As Beckett says, they consider that the provision of education should be the responsibility of the state! These new Academies sit alongside new 'trust schools' – schools within Local Authority jurisdiction but also with their own independent sponsors. The £2 million contribution from sponsors has also been dropped as a requirement since many had not paid it.

While it is true that some Academies have continued in the traditions of the inner-city schools they have replaced and have genuinely comprehensive intakes, others have become covertly selective and have deliberately tried to recruit from some sections of the population rather than others. The University College London sponsored Academy in Camden, for instance, located in one of London's most up-market residential areas and scheduled to open in 2011, claims its 1,000 students will benefit from 'a tailored programme of master-classes, seminars and summer schools given by UCL staff and supported by UCL students, and will have access to UCL's world class facilities, including its laboratories and libraries' (http://www.ucl.ac.uk/news/news-articles/0802/08022903). In comparison, the Local Authority network of Academies in Birmingham, where schools are sponsored by local employers, will concentrate on offering the specialist diplomas, creating a situation where, according to Richard Hatcher of the Anti-Academies Alliance, employers can 'pick and choose' their future workforce (www.antiacademies.org.uk).

If there is still any coherent rationale behind the programme, it would seem to be that of reducing – even further – the influence of the local community and teachers over their schools in the name of 'raising standards'. There is no clear evidence however that these have improved. While some Academies have claimed success, others have failed Ofsted inspections, even as 'failing schools' in the LA sector are still threatened with being shut and reopened as Academies!

Whatever happened to the learning society?

As part of his call for a 'Cultural Revolution' (*sic*) in the education system and as one of the key architects of the standards agenda, Professor (now Sir) Michael Barber pointed to 'disturbing evidence' about the extent of pupil disengagement as they progressed through secondary school (Barber 1996: 71). For Barber this was a major symptom of an under-performing education system. However, an irony of the 'standards agenda' is that, even though many students have continued to improve their performance in public examinations, they have not necessarily given a positive endorsement to their school and their teachers. If millions have been spent on the various National Curriculum 'strategies' alluded to in Chapter 1 and on helping teachers deliver the ideal lesson (with a clearly structured beginning, middle and end) while differentiating pupils to maximise learning outcomes, then for many practitioners, 'getting through the day' in the classroom continues to be a constant struggle. Invariably, after the examination body training courses that provide 'hints' to teachers on how to get their students through exams, it has been programmes that concentrate on 'behaviour management' that have been the most popular with most teachers signing up for INSET (Professional Development).

There is, for instance, little evidence that student behaviour has improved in the way that the government's 'behaviour tsar', Sir Alan Steer, would like to suggest. Querying Steer and Ofsted's findings that only 6 per cent of schools have behaviour problems, Dr Terry Haydn, a teacher trainer from East Anglia University, suggested that most teachers adapted their lessons to the need to control the class rather than focusing on achievement and claimed that talented and experienced teachers were still leaving the profession (*TES* 1 May 2009).

A motion on pupil behaviour topped the agenda of the National Union of Teachers' conference in 2008 and, more recently (April 2009), the Association of Teachers and Lecturers (ATL) – considered more moderate than the NUT but nevertheless also affiliated to the TUC – published the results of its own survey based on a sample of 1,000 teachers, lecturers and support staff. According to ATL, nearly one quarter of school and college staff have endured violence from a student. Over 40 per cent of respondents felt that student behaviour had deteriorated over the past two years and 58 per cent believed it had worsened over the past five years. 87 per cent of staff had dealt with a disruptive student during the 2008/09 school year. These manifestations and general low level disruption reflects collapse of the implicit promise of the past linking good behaviour in school with employment afterwards.

In less differentiated primary schools, the incidents reported by a third of respondents, compared to 20 per cent of teachers in secondary schools, may be linked to an impoverished 'underclass' with a teacher reporting physical abuse from pupils as young as five years old:

> I and other members of staff were physically assaulted daily by a five year old (including head-butting, punching etc). He was taken to the head to "calm down" then brought back to apologise.

It became a vicious circle. I was off sick as a result. People often underestimate that young children can be as violent and intimidating as the older ones.

The ATL also reported sixth form and FE teachers experienced higher levels of disrespectful behaviour in the classroom, with over 85 per cent of respondents reporting the use of mobile phones during class and in lectures, a common complaint in HE also.

According to the National Association of School Masters Union of Women Teachers (NASUWT), barely one in ten physical attacks on teachers or other pupils is reported to Local Authorities and as a result school safety was seriously at risk (*TES* 10 April 2009). The Union also found that one in six teachers had been physically assaulted and half had been verbally abused in the last two years (*TES* 10 April 2009). In a further report the ATL highlighted 'failing parents' as a major reason for its members' classroom problems. ATL General Secretary, Mary Bousted, used a full page spread in *The Observer* (5 April 2009) to urge parents to take more responsibility for the activities of their children rather than leaving it to teachers. The ATL also reignited what will be referred to later as the 'toxic children' debate by blaming televisions in bedrooms and play-stations, rather than material poverty, for children's poor attentive and oral skills in the classroom.

Blaming the parents however, avoids the need to look at the way in which students themselves perceive school. According to an OECD study, just over half the 15 year olds in UK schools say they are 'often bored' and time wasting at the start of lessons was reported by 41 per cent of 15 year olds, while 28 per cent said school is somewhere they do not want to go even to meet their friends – the main positive reason always given for attending. British students find school more boring than their peers in many of the 32 industrialised nations surveyed by the OECD (*Independent* 30 October 2002).

Meanwhile, truancy rates among pupils in England rose in 2008 to their highest level since records began. Nearly 230,000 pupils were classified as persistent absentees, meaning they missed more than 20 per cent of school. Overall, the number of missed lessons – including those lost to illness – decreased, but there were an estimated 63,000 unauthorised absences/ truancies every day – equating to 1 per cent of all school sessions missed without a valid reason (*BBC News 24* 26 February 2009). At its worst, dissatisfaction is demonstrated by the 400 arson attacks on schools every year (*Guardian* 4 April 2006). In another sign of the times, hundreds of schools have installed CCTV cameras in classrooms to show 'good practice' by teachers but also, as *The Guardian* (4 August 2009) quotes one school source to 'produce dramatic improvements in behaviour, improve concentration and productivity' with one headteacher claiming to have tripled GCSE results since cameras were installed.

Learning to Labour *for our times*

A vivid insight into what 'raising standards' means for some primary schools in inner-city UK today is given by anthropologist Gillian Evans' in her 2006 book *Educational Failure and Working Class White Children in Britain*. This particular demographic grouping was officially pronounced the lowest achieving of any group bar traveller children. That her book is set in a primary school in inner-London Bermondsey shows how much – and how little – has changed since Paul Willis wrote his account of Birmingham secondary schoolboys leaving school for a life of 'shit work' more than 30 years earlier.

Indeed, Evans begins by repeating Willis's question as she earwigs on a conversation between two shelf-stackers in Tesco and asks, 'Why hasn't education made any difference to these young people?' She finds the answer in the local primary school where 'the whole of the school day . . . is a battleground in which the fight to inculcate in children a disposition towards formal learning is waged against their more fundamental desire to play'. 'By virtue of her ability to hold the children's attention, to keep them still and quiet, the teacher's power and authority to impart knowledge is recreated on an hourly basis.' 'Exclusion from the group is her only weapon of restraint', since 'streaming can become subversive as children react against the demeaning position ascribed to them'. So 'a large measure of the teacher's and the children's emotional energy is preoccupied with the heightening tension caused by challenges to adult authority' as boys seek to assert their place in the parallel gang culture of the surrounding streets. And not only boys: 'it is a tragic indictment that a child like Emma is likely to leave primary school unable to read and write proficiently'.

Meanwhile, 'having no problem controlling their children at home, working-class parents are often frustrated at the teachers' inability to discipline their children at school'. This was Gillian's starting point as she noticed how differently her neighbours' children on the estate behaved at home compared with when they were at school. As she says, it is not that working-class parents do not care about their children, just 'that formal learning and caring tend not to be synonymous and often the expectation is that formal learning is what happens at school'. By comparison, 'Middleclass mothers, who are usually educated to degree level, take it for granted that formal-learning-type skills should be incorporated into the caring relationship with the child at home' and 'since middleclass people value education above all else', in a situation where 'the relationship between the social classes in England hinges on a segregation that is emotionally structured through mutual disdain' and 'at school, and in life, middleclass people behave as if they are doing working-class people a favour', their comparatively lower level of average educational attainment comes to be seen as a deficiency even by working-class people themselves.

'Rather than making their behaviour seem pathological', Gillian Evans explains 'how it is that young boys in certain kinds of social situations can come to structure their relations with one another in such a way that troublesome, violent and intimidating behaviours become a social good'. For 'as long as failing schools are protected from proper scrutiny and disruptive boys are treated as individuals with emotional and behavioural difficulties, the basis of the formation of their peer groups is neglected and the cycle goes on'. Meanwhile, 'the unobtrusive children, the ones who behave well but struggle to learn anything, continue quietly to demonstrate the fallacy that good behaviour means effective learning. Their lack of progress highlights the cost to the whole class of the teacher's continuous focus on trying to manage the disruptive boys'.

That school represents, as Gillian says, 'posh people's values' was sociological orthodoxy 30 years ago when school leaving and working class were synonyms and qualifications were a proxy for middleclass. Now the proxy for 'underclass' is free school meals. It is also an indication of how the all-through academic National Curriculum has intensified the situation from primary school on.

In these circumstances, the farce of SATs is well described since there is only one teacher 'who can induce this class, with its high proportion of disruptive boys, to apply itself to school work for any length of time. Christine's authority is a function of the trust she has nurtured in her relationship with the children . . . in particular the respect she has managed to gain of the core group of badly behaved boys'. A large part of Evans' book becomes a narration of this teacher's tragedy as she is ground between an ineffective management 'who have little or no teaching responsibilities' and the 'exhausting and dangerous place' that this 'failing' school has become. Because 'the teachers' first commitment is always to the children', Christine recognizes 'the failure of the school's inspection wouldn't do the children any good' as it would only end up being run by outside agencies and eventually close. Christine does not therefore reveal that the most disruptive boys are all suspended during the week of Ofsted's inspection and so 'her urgent need for support is missed and the failures of senior management are effectively concealed by the naïve collusion of the governing body'. In the end Christine leaves and the school will close anyway. The system is self-sustaining, policed by the Inspectorate in a perpetual process of crisis management inflicted on the long tail of failing primary and secondary schools.

African-Caribbean boys – a new educational underclass?

That some groups of students have continued to remain marginal to the education system is confirmed by the continued under-performance of African-Caribbean boys. While Paul Willis was describing the alienation of white working-class boys in the 1970s, Bernard Coard (1971) provided a graphic account of how many in the first generation of British-born African-Caribbean children were labelled as 'educationally sub-normal'. New Labour's standards agenda adopted a universal approach to raising performance, assuming all sections of society would benefit in the same way. It is true that many inner city schools have seen exam pass rates improve – in some cases, as we have seen, significantly, but how have African-Caribbean boys faired after over ten years of New Labour?

According to Janet Graham, currently researching African-Caribbean boys in inner city schools and now collaborating with Coard, nothing much has changed. The under-achievement of these boys, she maintains, is still a scandal and, according to Professor Gus John (2006), still a major indictment of the British schooling system. Graham argues that New Labour policies have not addressed cultural diversity and systemic and institutional racism in schools. She found that, just as in Coard's time when West Indian children were sent to what were then called Educationally Subnormal (ESN) schools, today African-Caribbean boys who had performed well in primary schools were, because of 'behavioural and emotional' problems, over-represented in Learning Support Units in secondary schools, more likely to be excluded than any other group and less likely to make the sixth-form. Black students as a whole (home and overseas) are also more likely to be in new universities rather than in elite institutions (see further).

The standards agenda's 'one size fits all' curriculum does not cater for the cultural and academic needs of groups like African-Caribbean boys. In many inner city 'multi-cultural' schools where white students are often in the minority, African-Caribbean boys have become a 'hidden' population, their specific needs lost in the 'school improvement' agenda. Graham also disputes claims that the failure of African-Caribbean boys can be explained by issues of poverty or 'bad parenting' – another New Labour obsession. Instead, Graham points out that, like everybody else, these boys want to pass their exams and get on in life. It is the school system that lets them down. For many African-Caribbean boys, she contends, leaving school at the statutory age is a one-way ticket to the street, to gang culture, crime and possibly prison or even getting killed. Young African-Caribbean boys whom Graham interviewed complained that some teachers were racist but most just didn't understand their culture and their situation in British society. It is therefore hardly surprising that, as she says, some Black activists have given up on reforming state education and demand separate classes or even separate Black schools.

Teachers in a right state

Chapter 1 outlined some of the changes to the job of teaching. The reality for practitioners has been an iron cage of micro-management with teachers – like pupils – doing what they are told when, following lesson plans and delivering centrally-determined learning objectives while having to justify how they spend their time in school and college. The standardisation of lessons, regardless of the subject being taught or the needs of students, has resulted in a huge increase in the number of 'competency' cases as practitioners are constantly monitored by line managers to ensure that they are delivering lessons correctly.

Despite the 'workload agreement' that guarantees a tenth of teachers' time for 'PPA' (planning, preparation and assessment) and limits the amount of administrative work that school teachers are supposed to undertake, union surveys continue to show teachers working more, not less. As a result, the NASUWT 2009 Conference voted to take industrial action in schools where the management did not comply in reducing their workload. Barber's vision of a new kind of twentyfirst century teaching professionalism (Barber 1996: 235) on which New Labour's remodelling was based, remains light years away from the Gradgrind realities of teachers' lives. So are the new 'para-professionals' Barber considered essential in modernising 'the teacherforce' for the twentyfirst century.

The NUT's 2009 Conference, opposed in principle to the use of unqualified 'cover supervisors', voted for action to restrict their use to absences up to three days in secondary schools and one day in primary schools. Rather than using 'higher level teaching assistants' who might at least have had some training in classroom management, schools are employing a variety of non-teaching and clerical staff to cover for absent teachers. One of the conference speakers shocked other delegates when he described a school in his area that had used a nightclub bouncer to cover lessons (*TES* 17 April 2009). Yet, according to researchers at London Metropolitan University, one in ten state primaries and 40 per cent of secondaries admitted regularly turning to support staff, who can earn as little as £6.50 an hour, to take classes – sometimes for a whole term (www.telegraph.co.uk 11 September 2009). In addition, a new code of conduct drafted by the General Teaching Council now requires teachers to 'maintain reasonable standards in their own behaviour that enable them to uphold public trust and confidence in the profession' – a weekend charter, 'practically demanding sainthood' (*Guardian*, 3 September 2009).

As the job of teaching increasingly resembles that on a production line, remodelling driven by the standards agenda has changed the relationship between teacher and taught. Classroom activity has become more intense with teachers, if not yet being expected to account for how they use every minute of every lesson, constantly 'teaching to the test'. As school students in Britain have become the most 'examined' ever, teachers are now undertaking a much higher assessment load than they have ever done before. Again, this parallels HE where numbers have expanded on a reduced unit of resource. It also follows FE where in 1997 Ainley and Bailey found lecturers who said they were 'too busy assessing students to teach them anything'!

Education by numbers

Rather than a new learning culture, 'education by numbers' (Mansell 2007) is a more appropriate definition – a performance culture continually under strain, if not at breaking point. Just as soon as one set of targets is achieved, new ones are immediately introduced and the stakes are raised again. Despite this 'continual improvement', as we have argued, perpetual increases in examination performance only lead to accusations of 'dumbing down' and consequently confidence in the system continues to wane. So much so that the Assessment Reform Group told the *Guardian*

(18 August 2009) that, because of their unreliability, raw scores published by government ought to be accompanied by a 'health warning'. Despite increased spending by New Labour, the OECD recorded that, with only 5.9 per cent of GNP going to education, Britain was below average for developed economies and in danger of falling further behind (*TES* 11 September 2009).

If this chapter has shown how the New Labour standards agenda ran out of steam, then an ICM poll for *The Guardian* (25 August 2009) showed Labour, for the first time falling behind the Conservatives in support for its education policies. Over 52 per cent of voters thought state education would be better under the Tories. The real crisis in education however, is much deeper and more fundamentally challenges both New Labour and Old Tory proposals for education. In 2009, a year when examination pass rates once again rose to record levels, the unemployment rate for young people also reached heights not experienced since the 1980s. In the next chapter, we argue that it is for this reason that education is now experiencing its own 'credibility crunch'. This can only further undermine its legitimacy as the mismatch between what it is assumed a young person with a particular set of qualifications can look forward to, and the realities of the labour market, become starkly apparent.

3

Overqualified and Underemployed

Introduction

The UK economy officially went into recession at the end of 2008, recording two successive quarters of negative growth for the first time since 1991. Using the Labour Force Survey (LFS) which counts the number of people looking for work, rather than the narrower Claimant Count of those actually signing on, the number out of work reached 2.4 million by the summer of 2009 – a 14 year high and an unemployment rate of almost 8 per cent. If the media initially characterised the downturn as a 'white collar' or 'middleclass' recession, because of the effect on the financial sector, the number of under 25s without work rose from 600,000 at the beginning of 2009 to 928,000 by the end of June – over 1 in 6 (*Guardian.co.uk* 13 August 2009) with some forecasts as high as 1.3 million by 2011 (www.centreforcities.org). Nearly 18 per cent of 16–24 year olds were now classified as NEETs – a total of 835,000 and up by 100,000 on the previous year (*Guardian.co.uk* 18 August 2009). Of the 115,000 added to the unemployment total in March alone, almost half (56,000) were under 25 (*Guardian* 13 May 2009). By June, the number of 16–24 year olds claiming Jobseekers Allowance had reached 456,000. While the Claimant Count figure is always lower, it should also be remembered that 16–17 year olds are normally not eligible for JSA. According to the OECD (*TES* 11 September 2009), 10.7 per cent of 15–19 year olds were out of work or education, while the July 2009 jobless statistics showed unemployment amongst the 16–24 age group up by another 20,000 – edging towards the one million mark with the inclusion of summer school and college leavers.

As suggested in Chapter 1, recent changes in employment patterns have meant that unemployment amongst young people has remained above average, particularly for those without qualifications. According to figures from the Prince's Trust (http://www.princes-trust.org.uk/) in 2002 at the height of the Blair boom, unemployment amongst 16–24 year olds was still 5 per cent with half of this group being without qualifications. As seen in our account of the 1980s, young people's prospects are much worse in recessions as many employers stop recruiting. Young workers are also likely to be the first to be laid off, costing employers less in terms of redundancy payments. As firms stop hiring the length of time taken to enter or re-enter the labour market after finishing a programme of education and training lengthens. In the recession of the 1980s, over a million young people – one in three – were registered as unemployed. However, the failed Youth Training Scheme persuaded millions of working-class students to remain in education beyond the compulsory leaving age. Today, many of the current generation have stayed in education often until their early 20s and now have nowhere else to go. According to Danny Dorling, who compiled the figures for the Prince's Trust, if the number of 18–25 year-olds on the dole exceeds a million in this recession, these leavers will be the hardest hit since the crash of 1929. He adds that if trends follow those of the 1980s recession, about 140,000 – or one in five – of this year's GCSE cohort will be claiming JSA by the time they are 21.

Unsurprisingly this time round the worsening economic conditions have again been reflected in a further increase in demand for places in full-time education post-16 and the government initially struggled to find the money to fund an extra 35,000 places in schools and colleges while cutting back on support for universities – 'the obscenity of freezing student places in a recession' (Nick Cohen in *The Observer* 12 July 2009). In March, schools and colleges were informed by the Learning and Skills Council that the budget for post-16 education in schools was being reduced by 3.71 per cent and in colleges by 2 per cent – a total budget shortfall of £200 million. The crisis over the 14-19 diplomas deepened as headteachers complained that they might not have the money to fund them (*Guardian* 7 April 2009).

Despite the 2009 budget showing government borrowing already escalating, Chancellor Alistair Darling came up with a £2.7 billion 'jobs and skills' package to promise that a generation of young people would not be 'abandoned to a future on the scrapheap'. Darling pledged to make good the underfunding of post-16 by proposing another 54,000 places in sixth forms and FE. As Mark Corney pointed out however (Corney 2009), even if the extra places were taken up, this would only represent a 3 per cent increase in those in full-time education and training. There were still, Mark indicated, almost 150,000 16 and 17 year olds in non-apprenticeship jobs and, as a result, at high risk of becoming unemployed.

By way of comparison to Darling, the Bank of England's Monetary Policy Committee member David Blanchflower recommended spending an additional £90 billion to keep young people in full-time education for a year or two (*Guardian* 13 April 2009). Blanchflower told BBC's *Newsnight* (21 May 2009) that with unemployment heading towards three million, 40 per cent were likely to be under-25 and represented a 'lost generation' likely to experience a 'scarring' effect for many years to come. Young people – even those with qualifications – are in a cruel double bind; they are in competition with older workers who have experience even if they lack qualifications. According to the National Apprenticeship Service, employers have been more sympathetic to older workers applying for apprenticeships, with 60,000 of the 224,000 entering schemes being over 30 (*Guardian* 23 June 2009).

Trying to convince a sceptical public that the government were at least doing something, Darling promised every young person under 25 who had been out of work for a year either a job or a place on a training scheme. The £1 billion Future Jobs Fund (www.dwp.gov.uk /futurejobsfund) would add up to 150,000 extra jobs. Most of these would be in the public sector where Local Authorities would be subsidised at up to £1,500 per head to take on 50,000 extra staff in 'social care' or other 'socially useful' work.

This was an offer that couldn't be refused since refusal would result in termination of benefits.

All NEETs now?

As the recession unfolded, the crisis of graduate unemployment was heavily exposed in the media, particularly in relation to the crisis in the financial services sector. While television featured footage of traders clearing their desks in Canary Wharf, narrowing graduate recruitment was reported with firms favouring 'the Magic Five' top universities (*Guardian* 10 January 2009) or, in the banking sector, even a 'Holy Trinity' of three (*Financial Times* 5 January 2009). The Association of Graduate Recruiters reported a quarter of graduate jobs lost with 48 applicants for every remaining post (*THE* 15 July 2009).

In early 2009 the government announced a package of measures to allow those graduating that summer – the first to have paid the £3,000 top-up fees – to work as 'interns' in the private and public sectors with universities and colleges arranging more than 2,000 internships and placements for new graduates. These often replace established graduate recruitment schemes but still count as graduate level employment. At the same time, a survey from the National Union of Students found that 80 per cent of undergraduates were 'concerned' or 'very concerned' about their future job prospects (*Independent* 9 April 2009) and a study by the graduate careers and recruitment consultancy High Fliers (www. highfliers.co.uk), based on face-to-face interviews with over 16,000 final-year students, found only a third believed they would start a graduate level job after leaving university.

The High Fliers' data showed that, despite the volume of applications from final year undergraduates increasing noticeably in 2009, the number of applicants who had been offered work commensurate with their qualifications had fallen by a third. Leading graduate recruiters reduced their targets for 2009 by 17 per cent since the latest graduate recruitment round began in September 2008. Employers in just two areas – the public sector and the Armed Forces – stepped up their graduate vacancies in both 2008 and 2009. As a result, there are now 51 per cent more entry-level positions for graduates in the public sector and 17 per cent more in the Armed Forces. A survey by the Chartered Institute of Personnel and Development reported in *The Observer* (21/06/09) claimed that nearly half of employers surveyed were not intending to recruit school leavers or graduates that summer. In August, British Telecom – the UK's ninth largest employer – announced it was closing its graduate recruitment programme as it continued to cut costs in the downturn (*Guardian* 24 August 2009)

Meanwhile the spring and summer of 2009 saw a huge increase in the number of advertisements for graduate 'internships', raising concern that – as with YTS 20 years before – employers were exploiting young people for cheap labour. In the most sought-after professions like journalism, the music industry, PR and advertising, they even expect interns to pay their own expenses, thereby excluding poorer graduates (*Guardian* 1 August 2009). Instead of moving *From School to YTS* (Ainley 1988), students were moving from university to internships and non-students from school to 'apprenticeships'.

A graduate education without graduate jobs

The increase in youth unemployment – a direct consequence of the recession – has intensified longer term changes in the relationship between education, qualifications and the labour market. It is the most pertinent example of a wider mismatch between qualifications held by the current generation and the opportunities to use them in the labour market. In this respect, the so called 'learning society' has more in common with what Randall Collins (1979) referred to as a 'credential society' and Ainley (1999) described as a 'certified' one.

Rather than Gordon Brown's 'endless opportunities', for many people education and training is increasingly like running up a down escalator – a situation where you have to gain more and more qualifications simply to stand still. This applies also to those in employment who have to train and retrain to maintain insecure positions. To describe the new normality now facing young people, sociologist Ken Roberts has used the term 'underemployment' (Roberts 2009a). Though Roberts applied this primarily to conditions in the new Eastern European economies, he considers underemployment to be the 'twentyfirst century global normality for youth in the labour market' (4). Roberts describes youth underemployment as possessing the following characteristics:

> High rates of unemployment (sometimes but not usually long-term). Employment in less than permanent, regular (official) full-time, full-paid jobs. Employment in jobs that fall well short of young people's qualifications and ambitions. (25)

The anticipated shift towards the dominance of the 'knowledge worker' has not materialised and there has been a significant over-estimation of the increases in highly skilled jobs required relative to those classified as 'unskilled' (Henwood 2003, who predicts 40 per cent of the fastest growing jobs in the twentyfirst century will be in the lowest quarter of the income spread). In our account of social mobility below, we argue that the current recession has accelerated the growth of services such as fast-food and in this respect we suggest we could be moving to a rather different shape of occupational structure to the one anticipated by Gordon Brown, one which we call pear-shaped. Phil Brown and Hugh Lauder (2006) have also contested the idea that low-skilled jobs would tend to migrate to low-waged areas of the world, while 'high skilled' employment opportunities would be integral to the continued success of the more wealthy countries. Instead, they suggest that many low-cost countries are now increasingly able to match, if not surpass developed countries in terms of the number of graduates they produce and employ.

The current recession is accentuating the longer term changes in employment patterns described in Chapter 1. For example, there is a drift towards part-time working for younger and older employees as an increasing proportion of older people continue working because of the way in which the downturn has damaged pensions and eaten into their savings. An 'ageing' workforce has obvious implications for young people seeking to enter the labour market and for relations between the generations.

According to the OECD (press release 8 September 2009), a male student who completes a university degree can still look forward to lifetime earnings of $186,000 – more in total than someone who only completes secondary education. This 'graduate premium' is much disputed but does not necessarily mean that graduates end up in graduate jobs. For example, as indicated more and more graduates report that they are overqualified for their current employment. As graduates move into non-graduate jobs, the wage levels of those with lower qualifications are also suppressed as they in turn are forced to take up lower paid work. If graduates are 'underemployed' then – as the OCED emphasises – young people without qualifications are more likely to be 'unemployed'.

Student fears about future employability emerged from the Department for Innovation, Universities and Skills own 'student listening programme' (*Independent* 10 April 2008). DIUS's report of the event (April 2008) highlights student concerns about the larger number of undergraduates and that post-graduate study was becoming increasingly necessary to maintain a competitive edge. According to *The Financial Times* (11 August 2008), one in three UK graduates are already in non-graduate jobs, with six out of ten art and design graduates over-qualified for their current occupations. Another third in the High Fliers' data reported that they would have to accept any job they were offered.

Elias and Purcell (2004) divided 'graduate jobs' into five types ranging from the 'traditional' to 'niche market': traditional graduate jobs include medicine, higher education and science (12 per cent); modern graduate jobs, eg. management and IT (13 per cent); new graduate jobs, eg. marketing and sales (16 per cent); niche graduate jobs, eg. leisure and sports management (21 per cent); non-graduate jobs (38 per cent). With so many working in this last category, a further tranche of jobs, in many parts of retailing for instance, may become open only to degree holders.

Once again, the recession is aggravating but not causing a situation where graduates increasingly end up in 'non-graduate' jobs and as a result set off a domino effect intensifying job replacement. As Mike Hill, Chief Executive of Graduate Prospects and the Higher Education Careers Service Unit, stated in a letter to *The Guardian*

(12 February 2009), 'As graduates have taken A-level jobs and in turn those with A-levels have taken GCSE-level jobs, the unqualified have nowhere to go.' Yet, while the 'relative' advantages of being a graduate might hold up and a 'labour queue' theory of employment continues to operate, this will not stop a fall in the ratio between graduate earnings and graduate costs as the balance between well-paid permanent employment and casualised 'Mcjobs' continues to tilt.

Indeed, McDonalds themselves have promised to provide 10,000 'apprenticeships' for counter staff, after previously introducing the 'Burgerlaureate' for supervisors and managers (Allen 2008). KFC plan to create 9,000 new jobs, Subway 7,000 and Domino's Pizzas – enjoying an 18 per cent increase in sales in the UK in 2008 – plan to double their franchise outlets (*London Metro* 17 February 2009 front page headline 'Jobs: Now UK is a fast food nation'.)

Even if they are being accentuated by the biggest recession since the 1930s, these disturbing trends suggest that the overall relationship between education and the economy and the argument for what we have referred to elsewhere as a 'new correspondence' (Allen and Ainley 2008: 7) is not the one that New Labour leaders visualised. Rather than the post-war 'pyramid' model of the occupational structure being replaced by one that is supposed to be diamond-shaped, with only a few at the top and bottom and the majority in the middle, the occupational structure has gone pear-shaped. It has become increasingly polarised with a 'working middle' competing more fiercely for a contracting number of professional/ managerial jobs at the top and growing numbers falling to the bottom. Rather than education facilitating social mobility, it has become a form of social security as people seek credentials to avoid falling into the growing 'underclass' at the bottom of society. We will return to this issue but in the meantime provide one more example of the lack of correspondence and hence dysfunctionality between education, the labour market and the economy.

Consolidation in HE, expansion in FE and training

Since New Labour came to office there has been almost a 30 per cent increase in the number of students starting university courses. After the Credit Crunch and as recession deepened however, it became clear that the expansion of higher education would be tempered. While continuing to officially promote the government's objective of a 50 per cent participation rate in higher education, John Denham, Minister for Innovation, Universities and Skills in a *Times* contribution (11 August 2008) defended the government's intention of increasing the number of young people entering apprenticeships to 29 per cent, arguing that 'higher education was not the only option for young people . . . and it is true that some young people would have been better advised not to go to university'. Corney (2009) also suggests that for many 16–17 year olds, particularly those without the qualifications necessary for higher education, becoming unemployed may be preferable to facing more full-time education. The CBI (2009) went much further calling for the scrapping of the 50 per cent target and the raising of fees.

Young people appeared not to be listening though. As the recession bit hard, applications to HE hit record levels with a 10 per cent increase in 2009. Many forwent their gap year to apply straight away before fees rose again and in the desperate hope that by the time they completed their degrees business would return to normal and their qualifications would be rewarded. Government reversed a previous decision to cut back on 'over-recruitment' to part-fund another 10,000 places in STEM subjects (science, technology, engineering and maths). Under pressure, it later increased this to 13,000 but, because it was not fully funded, not all universities – particularly in the Russell Group – took up the offer, preferring to protect 'quality' at the expense of quantity. HEFCE also continued to refuse to fund people returning for Equivalent or Lower Level Qualifications (ELQs).

As the summer progressed BBC News (24 August 2009) reported Universities and Colleges Admissions Service figures showing a record 611,947 university applications had been made, more than

10 per cent up on the previous year. On 29 August 2009, the Chair of the Million+ Group of universities, Professor Les Ebdon, told the BBC that 40,000 'extra well-qualified applicants' would not find places because the numbers had been capped. By the end of September, universities were told they faced fines for admitting beyond the cap (*Guardian* 26 September 2009).

Upskilling or reskilling?

The mismatch between qualifications and employment has been widened by the recession. This was illustrated by the discarding of much of the rhetoric associated with the 2006 Leitch Report and a new emphasis by government on 'reskilling' the unemployed rather than 'upskilling' the current and future labour force (*TES* 16 January 2009). According to the House of Commons Innovation, Universities, Science and Skills Sub-Committee, 'the climate has now changed' with renewed emphasis on 'training' rather than education. DCSF already signalled its intention to revamp the ailing Modern Apprenticeship, including introducing a new scheme for 14 and 15 year olds in 2008. This would be particularly for those considered to be 'academic failures' or even 'disruptive' – over 100,000 of whom already spend up to two days a week attending FE colleges as part of local Increased Flexibility Programmes.

Unlike the old-style apprenticeships referred to in Chapter 1 though, a place on a New Labour apprenticeship will not guarantee employment. Indeed, from the inception of John Major's Modern Apprenticeships in 1994 ('modern' because they were not legally time-limited and did not guarantee employment on completion) and similarly with the Diploma's new designation as 'applied,' rather than work-based, government has had problems persuading enough employers to offer them. As a result, as was the case with youth training some 30 years earlier, many apprentices are not 'employed' at all. Instead, they participate in 'programme-led' schemes run by a variety of providers including private sector training organisations as well as FE colleges. Like their previous counterparts on YTS, they receive an 'allowance' rather than a wage – apprentices must be paid a minimum of £95 from August

2009 (those on a 'wage' are able to earn up to £170 a week and should enjoy the same paid holidays as other workers). Leitch proposed 500,000 apprenticeships, while the government said it anticipated one in five school-leavers starting apprenticeships within the next decade (Department for Children Schools and Families 2008).

Before Darling's budget pledge to help the young unemployed, the government was already committed to fund 17,500 extra employer-led apprenticeship places (for which employers receive subsidies). Still there were reports of 'employed' apprentices being made redundant as the recession bit (*Guardian* 5 May 2009). With young people not on apprenticeships even more likely to face redundancy, the increase in programme-led schemes is almost inevitable. If this happens, it would represent a move back to 1980s *Training Without Jobs*, a return to the dual or 'European' model of education or training, rather than the American collegiate approach that has since superseded it. Divisions between those in full-time education and those who are not can only intensify some of the wider inequalities that have increased as the standards agenda has unfolded and which will continue to undermine its legitimacy.

Whatever happened to social mobility?

New Labour had sought to establish education as the main determinant of economic prosperity. In addition, as part of its efforts to consolidate a new consensus with young people, New Labour also emphasised the role that schools, colleges and universities would play in creating a new upwardly mobile society and a globally competitive 'knowledge economy'. In his Greenwich speech referred to in Chapter 1 and on the first page of the 2009 White Paper *New Opportunities*, Gordon Brown similarly compared the endless possibilities of the twentyfirst century with the post-war years 'when young people were held back by limited chances and limited room at the top'. If New Labour could not match Old Labour in its commitment to full employment and universal welfare, it could still appeal to its traditional base by offering to create a more socially just society through increased investment in education.

Yet there was little evidence for either absolute upward social mobility (when successive generations gain better jobs) or relative upward social mobility (when recruitment to top posts becomes more open but as many people move down as up). According to the White Paper itself (1.25), the proportion of people in higher and lower professions increased by 68 per cent between 1951 and 1971, resulting in extensive absolute upward social mobility. In contrast, between 1970 and 2000 the number of new 'higher skill' jobs being created remained more or less constant. Although higher than previously, this limited the amount of upward mobility (1.28) – with the number of men gaining better jobs than their fathers remaining roughly the same as in 1951–1971. Women gained however as they moved into 'professional' – or at least non-manual office and other positions – employment in the expanding services sector.

This lack of social mobility and increasing inequalities of opportunity between rich and poor presented a very different picture of the occupational structure to that conjured up by Blair and Brown. It is true that the post-war pyramid of non-manual middle over manual working class has been eroded by the applications of new technology and the expansion of services but it has been replaced by new inequalities and uncertainties. The fact that young people need to gain more and more qualifications simply to maintain their place in the occupational order is a reflection of this insecurity, where the aim is to avoid downward mobility into a new 'underclass' of temporary employment on minimal pay as much as it is to aspire to move upwards. Though still aspiring to join the professional/ managerial elite at the top of the occupational structure, most people remain trapped in the 'working middle' of society. Rather than the professionalisation of the proletariat, the reality has been a proletarianisation of the professions, especially as the same processes of automation and outsourcing that deskilled manual trades in the '70s and '80s have reached up the employment hierarchy to reduce many non-manual so-called professional and 'middleclass' occupations to the level of wage labour, ie. to jobs rather than careers.

New Labour claimed that the measures it put in place since 1997 and in particular the increased resourcing of education, would reverse these trends. However, rather than providing the opportunities for advancement that eluded the parents of many of today's current students, we argue that, on the contrary, with the chances for individual social mobility strictly limited and with the overall increase in professional and managerial jobs being nowhere near what government predicted, education has continued to remain a very unequal affair. Secondly, in the absence of traditional workplace divisions, education has been used as a means of social control – cementing old divisions while also creating new ones. While the world recession lingers, this will be even more the case.

The class structure goes pear-shaped

Stewart Lansley (TUC 2009) is one of many who challenge the view that the occupational structure has been transformed from the post-war pyramid model referred to earlier into a diamond shape. Instead of an expanding middle, he argues that there has been a 'hollowing out' of the middle from which many more fall to the bottom. Together with a steady rise in the earnings gap between rich and poor, this gives what we call a pear shape to the social structure. While it cannot be disputed that there has been an increase in the amount of white-collar employment (from 31 per cent in 1965 to 55 per cent in 2007) and a decline in the blue-collar sector, Lansley states that only 26 per cent of the population can be placed in the A and B (professional and managerial) occupational categories. Commenting on the nature of post-war social mobility, Lansley suggests 'those who have risen through the class hierarchy to swell the ranks of the "lower middleclass" have mostly ended up in a lower position by income distribution than where they would have been as members of the skilled working class a generation earlier' (10).

Lansley's arguments are based on an examination of income, rather than occupational titles. Though average or 'mean' income provided a figure of £463 per week in 2006/07, the income of the middle person 'median' came out at just £377. This was well behind the income of the top third of the population – the most common or 'modal' income being even less at a little over £200 per week. For those in the 'middling' jobs, which today require much higher levels of qualifications, the returns to education have been relatively small and as a result 'for a significant proportion, rising ambitions and expectations have been largely unfulfilled' (Lansley: 26). This also reflected the limited amount of social mobility with the 2009 White Paper and the 2008 discussion paper *Getting on, getting ahead* that preceded it, having to accept the findings of academic research that relative mobility both up and down the occupational structure had declined (as above).

Further figures released from the Cabinet Office confirmed the extent of inequality within the occupational structure, showing wide disparities in opportunities with 75 per cent of judges, 70 per cent of finance directors and 45 per cent of top ranking Civil Servants still being privately educated (*Guardian* 14 April 2009) compared to 7 per cent of the population as a whole. The decline in social mobility is confirmed by other sources. The LSE's Centre for Economic Performance, for example, in their 2005 comparison of *Intergenerational Mobility in Europe and North America* found that social mobility in Britain is lower than in Canada, Germany, Sweden, Norway, Denmark and Finland (Blanden et al.). And while the gap in opportunities between rich and poor is similar in Britain and the USA, in the USA it is at least static, while in Britain it is getting wider. *The Guardian* (8 May 2009) reported that since 2005 the poorest 10 per cent of households had seen a £9 fall in weekly income to £147 while the richest 10 per cent enjoyed a £45 increase to £1,033. One quarter of all UK jobs are low paid (defined as less than two thirds of the median wage) and one third of all UK jobs held by women are low paid (Keep 2009).

And the gender gap remains

Despite girls catching up with and now surpassing boys at every level of learning and in all subjects – at least in terms of exam scores – since the introduction of the National Curriculum in 1988, this is not the case in the board room. Women occupy just 34 of the 970 executive director positions at companies in the FTSE 350 index, according to a survey by Co-operative Asset Management (*Observer*

23 August 2009). Women fare slightly better in non-executive posts but still occupy only 204 of the 1,772 jobs available. Only four chairmanships are held by women, equivalent to 1.3 per cent of the total, and just nine women serve as chief executives, or 3 per cent. 132 of the companies surveyed, including Barclays Bank and Royal Bank of Scotland, are men-only zones, without a single woman at board level.

In the financial sector in 2009 the Equality and Human Rights Commission reported a 'gender gap' of 60 per cent in annual gross earnings compared with 42 per cent in the economy as a whole and fewer than half the companies questioned were making any effort to reduce the pay gap. In other lucrative occupations, like law for example, women solicitors remain under-represented at senior levels despite making up the majority of new entrants into the profession. Like medicine, where the majority of student doctors are now women, senior posts such as consultants remain occupied by men with a tendency for women to be relegated to General Practice.

In school teaching however, where the majority female teaching force has been blamed for boys' underachievement, a recent survey by headteacher organisations (*Guardian* 25 September 2009) found that 44 per cent of secondary heads were women with 70 per cent in primary. In FE where the largest curriculum areas, such as health and social care, business administration and visual and performing arts, are all populated by a majority of women students and teachers, there has been what Simmons (2008) describes as 'increasing numerical and cultural feminisation'. To a certain extent this is also the case in HE, although, as Leathwood and Read (2009) point out, there is still a long way to go. Jocey Quinn (2003) confirms that 'many of the new women students are channelled into less elite institutions. Many . . . are mature or part-time . . . they are over-represented in the Arts, Humanities, Education and subjects allied to Medicine, particularly Nursing, and still a minority in Science and Technology' (22). She finds that although 'women students construct the university as a "protected space" from external threats' (20) and 'universities can no longer be simply represented as male spaces', 'they still remain male dominated' (25).

'Good schools'

The ability of certain groups in the population to maintain their relative position at the expense of others and thus sabotage New Labour's policies for increased relative mobility, was facilitated by the way the standards agenda was implemented in schools. As we related, raising the general level of qualifications for the population as a whole was only one aspect of this. As significant has been the way in which differences between learners were maintained through the intensification of the 'internal market' introduced by the 1988 Act and perpetuated by Conservative and New Labour governments thereafter. Benn and Millar (2006) trace the introduction of what is often referred to as the 'choice and diversity' agenda to New Labour's second period of office from 2001. They argue that the rapid expansion of specialist schools and the encouragement of Academies represented a decisive 'new era' in the government's approach to secondary education in particular. This 'post-comprehensive' programme constituted a step back from the 1997 commitment to concentrate on 'standards' rather than 'structures'. Yet, as we have noted, since 1997 and before under the Tories but not so systematically, the school system has been run as *Education PLC* with constituent parts encouraged to compete against one another. However, Benn and Millar are correct in understanding the effect that this has had on increasing inequalities, how it has helped accentuate social and economic divisions between rich and poor and how the marketisation if not privatisation of parts of the service has been used as a 'driver' for more of the same (Benn and Millar: 13).

A business model of education also casts parents and students as consumers, shopping around for the best product. Central to Benn and Millar's concerns has been the way in which current schools' admissions practices are being used to recreate grammar: secondary modern divisions and to encourage parents to aspire to get their children into 'good' schools while at the same time creating a situation where for this to happen some schools would have to double their intake and others would have to carry surplus places or close. *The Daily Telegraph* (3 March 2009) estimated that of the 560,000 children seeking entry to state secondary schools for September 2009 one in six had missed their first preference school. It added that some were paying more than £2,000 in solicitors' fees to build cases against schools and Local Authorities that had refused them and that the number of appeals would top the 80,000 lodged in 2008. So far university admissions tutors have managed to avoid litigation, despite a series of high profile cases, as the same chase is replicated in higher education.

Of course, the major division between schools continues to be between private schools (known as 'Independents') and state ones. A notable feature of the 2009 A-level results was that Independents accounted for 50 per cent of A grades, while at GCSE level 53.7 per cent of exam scripts from private schools were awarded A or A*, compared to 17.3 per cent in comprehensive schools. In April 2008, *The Telegraph* provided figures showing 511,677 children attending schools belonging to the Independent Schools Council (ISC) which represents 80 per cent of privately-educated pupils. This was an increase of 0.8 per cent on the previous year and a record high. Competition to get into the best state schools and the introduction of 'lotteries' in some areas had, *The Telegraph* reported, driven more parents towards fee-paying schools. On the other hand, less of them can afford the often exorbitant fees.

Still, according to Steve Machin of the London School of Economics (reported in *The Guardian* 29 January 2008), the percentage of children in independent schools in England is creeping back up to levels not seen since the 1960s. This is not only because the schools have regained the share lost following the economic difficulties of the early 1990s but is also a wider consequence of the changing role of educational qualifications in the labour market. It reflects a situation described earlier where social aspiration replaces rational preference for one school over another as the main driving force of parent 'choice'. The figures also reflect stark regional differences. In the north-east, just 4 per cent of children attend private schools, while in inner London it is nearly 16 per cent, in Bristol 20 per cent. Broadly, there's a strong north-south divide.

Recession-hit parents will predictably intensify competition for the 'better' state schools. Yet data from the Independent Schools Council (*TES* 1 May 2009) showed that, despite the average boarding fee increasing to £23,250 per annum, the number of students attending appears to have held up. Certainly those at the top of the Headmasters' Conference (HMC) pecking order, with fees well above average, are unlikely to be really affected and will continue to act as the Royal Road to elite recruitment via the selecting universities. According to *The Telegraph* (20 April 2009), pupil numbers held firm during the 1990–92 recession. It was not until the end of the recession in 1992 that they began to decline, with further small falls in 1993 and 1994. If that pattern were to be repeated, one would not expect private pupil numbers to fall appreciably until 2010, although there are already associated increases in home schooling and tutoring.

Faith in the system

If the gap between private and state schools continues to be the most significant division, within the state sector many church or 'faith' schools now constitute part of a new state elite. Successfully securing a place at a church primary vastly improves the chances of entering one of the top, generally single-sex church schools in the secondary sector. Again, according to *The Telegraph* (26 February 2008), hundreds of primary schools across the country are over-subscribed but figures obtained from Local Authorities show there are huge differences between schools, with two-thirds of primaries experiencing no competition at all. By contrast, in the newspaper's list of the 120 most oversubscribed primaries, more than a quarter were Church of England or Roman Catholic primaries.

Though they are supposed to conform to the requirements of a national school admissions code, faith schools – along with foundation schools and Academies – control their own admissions. Sir Philip Hunter, the chief adjudicator for schools admissions, revealed in his 2008 annual report that half of faith, foundation and academy schools had breached the code in some way, mainly on technicalities, with faith schools among the worst offenders (*Guardian* 3 October 2008). His study of all 150 Local Authorities in England and more than 3,000 faith schools, found more than 3,600 state schools in total breaking the code.

Research by Anne West and colleagues at the London School of Economics reported in *The Times* (3 March 2009) confirmed faith schools amongst the worst offenders. The admissions code bans interviews but there was evidence of schools inviting parents to meet the headteacher and of a significant number of faith schools still asking direct questions about parents' marital status. Hundreds of secondary schools have become 'specialist' schools but while few exercise the option of selecting up to 10 per cent of their students according to aptitude in the chosen specialist area, faith schools are more likely to do so. According to West, schools that are their own admission authority are, in theory, in a position to 'cream skim'. In other words, rather than parents choosing schools, schools are choosing the applicants who will maximise their league table results.

Alongside top faith schools, there are state schools that remain openly selective. There are 164 remaining grammar schools in England in ten Local Authorities. In Kent and Buckinghamshire more than 25 per cent of secondary students are educated in grammars and admitted on the basis of entrance tests at 11-plus. These schools hold their own in the league tables for top schools based on performance at A-level. On coming to office, New Labour committed itself to 'no more selection'. It passed legislation requiring a local parental ballot to take place before a grammar school be abolished but so far, only a single and unsuccessful ballot has taken place – in Ripon, North Yorkshire.

14-19 divisions: the recurrent crisis of vocational education

If *Choice and Diversity* increased the ability of 'successful' schools to differentiate themselves, 'diversity' was also increased as a result of the way that the 14-19 curriculum was organised. New Labour inherited a 'pathways' approach to 14-19 having built on, rather than challenged, the ideas in Sir Ron Dearing's National Curriculum/ post-16 qualifications review for the previous Conservative government. The new specialist diplomas referred to in Chapter 2 were a continuation of this process. As has been the case with previous vocational/ applied qualifications like the General National Vocational Qualifications, the take up of the diplomas has been restricted to schools that can still be considered to be relatively 'comprehensive' in intake and to FE colleges serving mostly working-class students, many of whom have been failed by tests and examinations in the academic National Curriculum.

As we have argued elsewhere (Allen and Ainley 2007 & 2008), since the collapse of real vocational apprenticeships and contrary to government rhetoric, the emergence of 'vocational' courses in the upper years of secondary education has had little relation to the development of workplace skills but is a way of dividing learners remaining in full-time education and training as a result of the absence of work. As staying on has increased so have the efforts of governments to divert students away from GCE A-levels and into vocational courses. In this respect they were unsuccessful – as we noted in Chapter 2; enrolment in A-level courses continued to rise whilst many other students used vocational qualifications as an alternative route mainly into the new universities. Following concern from HE about the difficulties of ensuring consistent standards, vocational qualifications suffered 'academic drift' (Burgess and Pratt 1974). GNVQs, for example, were redesignated 'applied' A-levels. Alienating many of the very students they were originally designed for, while not attracting those who continued to sign up for academic A-levels, entries fell. As a result, the 'vocational streams' that Dearing intended failed to establish themselves, leaving the prediction of the 2005 14-19 White Paper, that up to 40 per cent of 15–16 year olds would enrol on diplomas, looking increasingly unrealistic.

As yet, no private or grammar schools have made any definite commitments or joined any of the local consortia offering the diplomas, concentrating instead on academic education. Although the majority of universities, including Russell Group members, have declared they would recognise the diploma as an entry qualification, there is of course a huge difference between a qualification being 'recognised' and a student being offered a place. Even if, as claimed, Cambridge University may consider the new Engineering diploma a superior qualification compared to what currently exists, the overall situation is likely to be perpetuated rather than challenged by the new diplomas.

Unable to compete with school sixth forms and sixth-form colleges, many general FE colleges have long since abandoned A-levels altogether. The fact that in order to qualify for full funding, FE colleges have to provide a disproportionate number of 'skills based' Level 1 and Level 2 courses, including the new diplomas, only increases the difference with school sixths and sixth form colleges leaving general FE colleges in danger of becoming 'tertiary moderns'. The New Labour government was reported to be working with Lord Baker, the architect of Mrs Thatcher's National Curriculum and sponsor of the original City Technology Colleges (see Beckett 2007), to develop a network of technical schools sponsored by local universities, which would concentrate on offering the 14-19 diploma and 'train teenagers to become builders, technicians and engineers' (*Guardian* 31 August 2009). This initiative being promoted through the Academies programme and likely to be equally attractive to an incoming Tory administration, would indeed take us back to the three tier divisions of 1944.

A new elitism: the case of the Cambridge Pre-U

In fact, rather than swapping A-levels for diplomas, the concern about A-level standards has led a number of elite schools to break with A-levels and turn to new forms of certification such as, for example, Cambridge International Exams' Pre-U. As the first 'gateway' of specialist diplomas got off to a shaky start in 2008, the Pre-U was being piloted in 65 schools, mostly in the private sector. According to the Headmaster of Eton, 'Pre-U will offer pupils more stimulation and a system of testing that rewards creativity and lateral thinking' (*Times* 20 November 2006) while in the same article, the Head of Dulwich College, suggested the Pre-U represented a return to the original idea of A-level as a qualification for university entry.

There are other reasons however for Pre-U's emergence. Being primarily designed for academically high-performing students, many will consider the new qualification unashamedly elitist and – with A-level pass rates reaching 97 per cent and with 1 in 4 candidates now receiving an A grade – that its main purpose is to ensure the leading and most expensive schools can maintain their 'positional' advantage. As noted, private schools are still able to ensure a disproportionate number of top grades at A-level – 50 per cent of all A grades in 2009, even if state schools are closing the gap at B and C grades (*Guardian* 20 January 2009). More than half of GCSEs taken by private pupils also rate A*-A as compared with 17.3 per cent at non-selective comprehensives (*Guardian* 27 August 2009). Yet, elite schools clearly don't consider they can rely on the new A* A-level grade due to become available from 2010. In its place, Pre-U principal subjects will have nine different grades. At the top, will be Distinction 1, 2 and 3. At least one school, Charterhouse (fees £26,000 per annum), has decided to offer the Pre-U in some individual subjects rather than as a diploma, thus creating a brand of 'super A-levels'. This will mean, as *The Telegraph* (23 January 2008) reassured its readers, that private schools are 'likely to tighten their grip on leading universities'.

Of course, as Cambridge International Exams make clear, there is nothing to stop state schools introducing the Pre-U, particularly in individual subject areas where they may have expertise and especially since QCA have given it official backing. Fifteen of the schools teaching the new qualification from last September may be officially part of the state sector but all but two are grammar schools and one is a Jesuit boys' school and the other a girls' convent school. CIE claimed that 30 comprehensives would be part of the 2009 cohort (*Guardian* 11 November 2008); however, many comprehensive schools struggle to provide a variety of A-level and vocational options and simply won't have the resources to offer parallel courses in individual subjects.

There have always been alternatives to A-level. For example, the International Baccalaureate (IB) remains an established qualification, popular in International Schools but also attracting a small following in the state sector. Until 2009 at least, government, as part of its drive to promote 'diversity', was committed to ensuring the IB would be available in at least one school or college in every Local Authority, earmarking £2.5 million for this purpose. Now, with the emergence of the Pre-U, the further expansion of the IB is less certain. As well as being a more direct 'national' alternative to A-level, which according to Charterhouse has 'had its day' (*Telegraph* 24 January 2009), the full Pre-U is also much easier to deliver as it has a much smaller core component.

Mass universities for the many: elite universities for the few

The Pre-U seeks to occupy pole position in an increasingly complex landscape of post-16 certification where with mass participation HE, new types of correspondence between qualifications and institutions are evolving. Pre-U aims to establish itself as the flagship qualification for entry to the internationally selecting 'Ivy League' Russell research-based universities, leaving A-levels as a 'middle' qualification (maybe for the 94 Group of nationally recruiting campus-based mainly teaching universities); while vocational/ applied qualifications, including the new specialist diplomas – if they ever took off – may suffice for entry to the local and (sub) regional 'clearing' (Million+) increasingly training universities.

Competition to obtain a place in the UK Ivy League will only be intensified by the recession which will lead to a decline in the employment prospects for 'other' graduates who until very recently were relatively recession proof but excluded from elite recruitment. As stated they are now facing a combination of higher underemployment/ unemployment, 'graduatisation' of another band of jobs and internships. As Roberts (2009a., 162) argues, 'graduates discover their qualifications do not guarantee middleclass jobs – merely admission to the pools that are allowed to compete for these jobs'. According to Sally Power and Geoff Whitty (2009), while 19 per cent of graduates from elite universities earned over £90,000 p.a., only 5 per cent of those who attended 'new' universities did so. Similarly, Francis Green and Yu Zhu reported *Increasing Dispersion in the Returns to Graduate Education* in 2009.

An additional type of differentiation within the HE sector is the two-year Foundation 'degree' covering specific vocational or occupational areas and designed for those at associate professional level – including the Higher Level Teaching Assistants in schools referred to in Chapter 2. While originally aimed at part-time or 'twilight' adult students, F'd's have since increasingly aimed at 18+ year olds and been franchised out to FE colleges. Especially with the proliferation, particularly in the post-1992 universities, of various types of Business Studies and IT courses, the vocational/applied pathway described earlier has been extended into HE.

All of this costs indebted students more in what has become a market currently differentiated for home students mainly by length of course – from two year Foundations to five or six year medical degrees and stretching on to the free market in full-cost postgraduate qualifications. This market, with its various higher education institutions offering different specialisms, offers schools and colleges a model to follow. For customers the principle is 'buyer beware' as the best informed and advised make the best choices they can afford. If at the end you find you still don't have a job, then you have only yourself to blame for choosing the wrong course. Your only option is to invest your remaining human capital more wisely on another course or training scheme. This market in which fees function as *de facto* vouchers only awaits completion by uncapped undergraduate fees differentiated by subject and institution. This will end the pretence of equality of outcomes across HE but reveal the reality of differentiation by cost.

Paying more for less

Although, as related, introducing tuition fees contradicted the government's goal of 'widening participation', New Labour broke its 2005 electoral promise not to raise fees further by allowing them to rise to a maximum 'capped' at £3,000 a year. As a concession, this sum was no longer paid up-front but repayable after graduation and after the graduate received a salary over a minimum income threshold. This saddled students with debts variously estimated to vary by course and institution from between £10,000 and £20,000. (See next chapter.) In another concession to widespread opposition, means-tested but reduced grants were restored in 2006 in a year that saw a 15,500 decline in the number of applications for the first time in eight years (although an increase in Scotland where the former system continued). However, despite dispro-portionate falls amongst adult, minority ethnic and working-class applicants – precisely those for whom government intended to 'widen participation' – the overall reduction of 3.1 per cent was less than predicted. Like the increased demand for HE as a result of the recession, this was also seen as 'success' by government and by the Russell Group of universities as a warrant for raising fees further.

Despite pressure from the (misnamed) Office for Fair Access, which joined with Russell Group universities to tell the govern-ment that the cap should be raised to £5,000 (*Guardian* 23 May 2009), New Labour delayed any decision about raising or uncap-ping fees until after the 2010 election. All HE institutions are already ranked in a hierarchy the poles of which are moving apart, as described above. The tertiary tripartism that has emerged repli-cates the old private, grammar and modern secondary tripartism.

Though more and more 'full-time' students rely on 'part-time' employment, as we will argue in Chapter 4, differentiation is aggravated by the number of students who, generally attending former-polytechnics and their associated FE colleges, now live at home in order to save money. Here also disabled, dyslexic and other students in most need of support are concentrated with the least resources available for them. This cultural difference of work-ing/ home and non-working/ away heightens what were already very different campus cultures. In addition, post-graduate and longer courses, such as medicine, largely restricted to the research-ing universities, cost more and so can only be taken by those who can afford them. Competition is leading to a process of what Leys (2001) called 'market-managed consolidation' in which 'weaker' institutions and 'vulnerable' departments within them merge or close. With public spending cuts impending whoever wins the 2010 election, a shake-out of institutions can be anticipated, especially in 'over-provided' areas like London. Many HEIs have already frozen recruitment and introduced voluntary redundancy schemes – just like FE after 1993.

This shake-out will coincide with the retirement of the '60s gen-eration of academics. Their departure is eagerly anticipated by Vice

Chancellors who, having got rid of 'the whingers' as they see them, can then introduce the four term years and two year degrees that are already being piloted at Plymouth University and elsewhere, following the UK's only private University of Buckingham. They hope this will ensure the survival of the lower level institutions below the redrawn binary line in HE.

The same qualification inflation/ diploma devaluation affecting all areas of education and training has, we have seen in HE, been associated with its feminization – if not yet 'feminismization' (Leathwood and Read 2009). The government target of widening participation to one half the age range is likely to be met for women if not for men. The ratio of female to male undergraduates equals three to two (David 2009), although more evenly balanced in what *The Times* guide calls 'The Good Universities'. So out of the 49.2 per cent of female 18–30s to whom participation had been widened by 2008/9, compared with 37.8 per cent of males, 50.6 per cent were in 'The Good Universities' while 62.5 per cent were in the bad ones. Just as – shameful statistic – there are more minority ethnic students at London Metropolitan University than in all 12 of the Russell Group universities (Archer et al. 2003). The general rule thus holds that the higher status the university, not only the older is it likely to be (with the exception of Warwick that proves the rule) but – with some exceptions in a few subjects – the whiter, younger, more male and more middleclass its students.

These class, gender and ethic disparities will be aggravated and engrained by the anticipated rise in fees in 2010 that an Oxford University spokesperson rejoices is 'almost inevitable' (*Times Higher* 23 July 2009). They are confirmed by institutional linkages between schools and colleges feeding poorer and less qualified students to vocational courses in local new universities, as Pugsley (2004) showed in a detailed study in South Wales where there was also a national dimension to the basic class determinant. This tendency would be further institutionalised if the suggestion of the Parliamentary Sub-Committee on Universities were implemented to exempt students who remain living at home from fees in exchange for abolishing their right to maintenance loans (*Guardian* 20 July 2009).

Widening to what?

Nevertheless, and despite the indebtedness involved, widening participation was a very popular policy – especially with parents who saw their children getting the opportunities for a higher education they never had. 'But my parents don't know what it's like!' many students add (Ainley 2008: 2). Even when formal study allows genuine intellectual development, educational participation starts from the largely instrumental motive of gaining labour market credentials. At all levels, this is recognised as 'overschooling' when school, college and university graduates fail to find employment comparable to the level of qualification they have acquired as the value of this level of qualification declines. Graduates' inability to capitalise on their investment in time and money leads to the conclusion that *'Education make you fick, innit?'* (Allen and Ainley 2007). Consequently, there is the crisis of legitimacy for young people and their teachers that we have emphasised at all levels of learning with regard to the education they are receiving and have received.

In HE, this crisis of legitimacy is instanced in part by growing student concern about costs, especially for those entering the expanding debt culture for the first time. As above, living at home whilst studying saves on costs; so does working while studying, though students often become trapped in a vicious circle of working long hours in 'Mcjobs' they are trying to escape from by studying, so reducing their final results and lessening their chances of escape. So too, as we have argued, does the graduatisation of jobs previously not requiring degree-entry qualifications, eg. in retail. Since their study has minimal intrinsic interest for many students, the exercise then becomes pointless. Instead of academic degrees many turn to vocational courses offering 'standards-based' 'skills for employability' but these reduce skill to competence, making large parts of HE even more like FE.

It was Utopian to expect the missionary efforts of higher education to transform society by widening participation and the consequences of this misconception are now becoming clear. In part this 'utopian capitalism', as Bourdieu called it (2003: 84), was bolstered by the promises of new Information and Computing

Technology. Typically, technological determinism celebrated the power of the machine and/ or of the (young) human mind with which it was supposedly uniquely associated and which was apparently able to 'multi-task' – facilitated by the machinery – in a way that ignored the 'focal awareness' required to create any real *Personal Knowledge* (Polanyi 1969). As a result, students at all levels have been overwhelmed with information that they lack the knowledge to order and represent.

They have not been helped to make sense of their situation by the fashion for academic postmodernism amongst many of their teachers which, from the 1980s on, complemented the commodi-fication of mass culture by celebrating an inability to construct a coherent argument or produce evidence in support of a hypothesis. The humanities and social sciences have thus largely retreated into new 'discourses' of fragmented incomprehensibility which are no more capable than traditional academic empiricism of questioning the purposes to which they are put or the society that uses them because, as Robertson explained (1994: 332), students 'can never be aware of the global totality of things'.

Students collect what they hope will be interesting and relevant courses assembled from the modules on offer in the academic marketplace but these do not necessarily cohere to make more than fragmentary sense of their experience. Like the more directly vocational programmes of study, such as the Business Studies degrees now taken by one in seven of all undergraduates, they are collections of modules which may or may not find an applica-tion in employment and rarely make any intellectual sense in themselves or cohere to constitute a meaningful overview of their field. Perhaps it is for these reasons that the high rates of course non-completion (from 2 per cent at Cambridge to 28 per cent at London Met.) are reflected most in the non-completion of 'voca-tional' courses. Only the elite, falling back on traditional exams for entry and graduation, develop a sense of overall understanding, at least within their often narrow and empirical area of specialisation but at the cost of academic obscurantism and an inability to com-municate their knowledge to others or to usefully apply it. This is often half the point of this further cultivation of cultural capital at this level however!

Alienated learning

At all levels of learning, in the absence of any practical context in which to apply what has been learnt, the identity of learners becomes the object of (ex)change independent of any use value. This creates a situation where learning becomes an end in itself – and a dead end at that! – rather than a means toward achieving employment, let alone enlightenment. The result is profoundly alienating for teachers and students alike as education turns into its opposite, foreclosing possibilities of learning in pursuit of the next examination hoop to jump through that certifies only ability to pass on to the next stage. This results, as Lave and McDermott write (2002), following Marx (1844), in:

> Alienated learning . . . "external to the learner", not freely undertaken. In his work, the learner does not ". . . affirm himself but denies himself, does not feel content but unhappy, does not develop freely his physical and mental energy but mortifies his body and ruins his mind". It is activity experienced as suffering. Alienated learners are only themselves when they are not learning . . . Such learning does not satisfy a need: it is coerced, forced, and a means to satisfy needs external to it . . . It is a loss of self.

This is profoundly disillusioning, as this new university third year undergraduate reflected in 2009:

> I never gave things in education the attention they deserved and I still don't now. Me having a somewhat low confidence and my belief in a formal, everyday, mainstream education has led me to university – the biggest mistake of my life. I can see why people come to university but the stories you hear about wild parties and "making the friends you'll keep for the rest of your lives" hasn't happened to me. My motivation and desire to be at university died at least a year ago and I don't really learn at university anymore. I haven't for a while. All I do is enough – enough to pass assignments, enough to say to myself I've done good enough so my parents don't think I'm wasting my time and money, which I have done. I truly feel that the best thing traditional, mainstream

education has taught me is that traditional mainstream education is not the only route to success. I grew up believing that an office job was the best job to have, like the stock-brokers in the city and although this is a very good dream to have, it shouldn't have been my only dream.

He speaks for many and yet his situation would be widely supposed to be better than most of those who were alienated from education much earlier on.

On the margins of inclusion

Alienated learning today begins for many in primary school as we saw with Gillian Evans' ethnography. By the time many young men (especially) leave school – if they last that long, David Smith (2005) provides similarly typical examples of social exclusion on the South London St. Helier Estate, built from the 1930s on as an overspill from inner city areas like Bermondsey for commuting industrial and office workers but now separating into private and residual public housing for employed owner occupiers and unemployed tenants. There one Job Club attendee recalled:

> I left school at 16 because I had a job lined up in a bakery . . . the job had been promised to me for years so I knew where I was going, work in a bakery, learn the ropes, get a loan and start up on my own. I soon found out there was no money in bread, all the little bakeries are closing down, being taken over by supermarkets else you've got chains buying up the family-run places and turning them into cafes . . . The business went under and all I knew was the bakery trade and the only jobs going were in supermarkets. [In] little places you get to learn everything: baking, ordering, doing the tills, icing, the lot. In a supermarket you just do the one job, baking the bread or serving and I didn't like the look of it. (94)

As Smith comments:

> Practically all of those interviewed had considerable experience of working in entry-level jobs in the formal economy after leaving school. However, few of these early jobs had resulted in stable

reasonably paid work, the typical trajectory being into work patterns increasingly characterised by short-term, low-paid jobs.
Sheltered from the realities of their local labour market location
through the support of family and local networks that provided
alternative sources of employment in the unregulated economy,
their early work histories reveal a succession of short-term employment. (95)

His study details 'a generational shift' (91) starting with 'the largely
unqualified cohort who entered the world of work between the
early 1980s and mid-1990s and was socialised into the lower
echelons of an emerging "post-industrial" labour market' (90). 'As
the number of low-wage and precarious jobs has increased following the recovery of the mid-to-late 1990s, working patterns have
become steadily fragmented and many have never fully recovered'
(94). For many since this YTS generation, 'bouts of unemployment
are experienced not as an interruption to work, but as a normal
feature of insecure and precarious employment' (90). We follow
Roberts in seeing this as a generalised condition of youth today
but one which especially afflicts Dorling's first lost generation of
the 1980s, or their children today (Dorling 2010). Even if there
is an economic recovery, another generation will be 'lost' as the
economy similarly restructures itself, adding another layer to the
misery; unless, of course, a very different path can be taken.

Youth in a right state

Collective solutions are not easy when people are so separated
from one another and do not share any sense of their situation.
If, New Labour's educational project for schools, colleges and universities left youth as a whole overqualified and underemployed,
then this chapter has shown that it has also increasingly divided
them. Young people are split between students (mainly girls) and
'apprentices' (mainly boys). Apprenticeships – if and when they
materialise – divide between employed and programme-led with
many dropping out to NEET 'Status Zero'. Students are in turn
divided by the tripartite hierarchy of institutions they attend and

the subjects they study, as well as by whether they continue to live at home or move away (even if returning after graduation). As we have predicted, these divisions will be heightened by the anticipated rise in student fees and the way that the main groups of universities – the antique Russells, the campus-based 94 Group and the local Million+ Group – are positioning themselves to compete for students in the marketplace.

The traditional student lifestyle is available to those who can pay for it whichever institution they attend but those who work their way through university can least afford it. As folklorist Matthew Cheeseman, studying the interactions of Sheffield and Hallam students, comments:

> If young working-class students agree to entertain significant debt on top of part-time work, then they can share in the student social experience of the middleclass, commercially packaged as this often is. If they choose to live at home with their family, they still go out and consume alcohol to comparable levels but they do this with non-students at other times and in other places to traditional students. (personal communication)

We therefore disagree with Roberts that there is one normative student experience in comparison with those who are not students. (We return to this discussion in the next chapter.)

In Chapter 1 we referred to recurrent government concern about those Not in Employment, Education or Training (NEET). Originally calculated to be anywhere from 9–13 per cent of the cohort, the dramatic increase in youth unemployment can only result in the consolidation of this new youth 'underclass' stigmatised as 'chavs'. Education and training policy, as much as what has happened to public housing together with (un)employment, has contributed through vocational courses for 'worthless' certification to the regional and racial segregation of this resurrection of the 'rough' and unskilled section of the traditionally manually working class. It now stretches to include many of the 30 per cent of 16+ year olds who fall considerably short of the 5 A*-C GCSE threshold, thus being excluded from advanced level courses and higher education and rejecting 'apprenticeships without jobs'.

These divisions amongst young people are ideologically justified by the apparently objective academic assessments that create and sustain them. Young people who have been failed by the system can thus believe that there is something wrong with them or they blame themselves for making the wrong choices. At the same time, they are repeatedly told that if they just try hard enough anyone can succeed. Exemplary role models are paraded before them to persuade them that this is the case but these are exceptions which prove the rule. Such moral exhortation only makes those who cannot live up to it feel guilty and hopeless. Chapter 4 will argue that these divisions can only intensify the problems of 'transition' to adulthood faced by what the media was quick to call 'the lost generation' of young people at the beginning of the twentyfirst century.

4

Lost in Transition or Transition Lost?

Introduction

The changing relationship that we have outlined so far between young people, education and employment has dramatically altered the situation of youth in society and relations between the generations. Chapter 1 recalled that in the post-war welfare state period the youth of the industrial manual working class went through a clearly defined process of 'transition' to adulthood. This involved a series of specific events – leaving school and starting work, leaving home to marry and have children. These usually happened in quick succession if not simultaneously. Amongst these transitions, apprenticeship with day-release to college was the only further formal learning undertaken after leaving school by a substantial minority of overwhelmingly young white working-class men, although nursing and some office work could offer an equivalent way forward for young working-class women.

By contrast, many of the sons and daughters of professional and managerial/ white collar/ non-manual workers, joined by a select few working-class children, remained in grammar and other academic schooling. They stayed on at school for an extra year to take exams and then increasingly an additional two years in sixth form with a growing proportion progressing to higher education. Even if 'going away' to college or university, they remained 'dependent' on their parents for longer. They returned to the family residence between terms and then often for what was generally a short period between finishing their studies and entering the labour market to sustain their own families through a salaried career. The role of a housewife and mother, combined with part-time work, remained an option for many working and middleclass women dependent upon their husbands' 'family wage' or salary, as compared with today when most couples both have to find employment to maintain a household.

Now that remaining in full-time education or training to 18 has become generalised and will become compulsory and with nearly half continuing to HE, the majority of young people experience a 'delayed transition'. This 'extended moratorium' now stretches between a childhood whose boundaries are also shifting and – for most – ever receding independent partnership and family formation sustained by employment. This involves a prolonged period of dependency on their parents or carers coupled uneasily perhaps with protracted relationships with their peers. At the same time there is a counter-tendency for children to grow up earlier physically and socially with periodic proposals for this to be officially recognised, for instance by an extension of the franchise to 16, following lowering of ages of consent, etc. But the age of 'maturity' if not majority has actually risen so that, as *The Observer* (21 June 2009) put it, '35 is the new 25'. Some sociologists have even described a new stage of 'emerging adulthood' (Cote and Bynner 2008) with young people, particularly in the cities of North America and Europe, suspended in a perpetual *Friends* situation, like the cast of the long-running 1990s TV sit-com (now endlessly repeated!). Roberts (2009a), as we have noted, finds *Youth in Transition* in Eastern Europe pioneering this tendency before those in the West.

This chapter will argue that declining employment opportunities, the increased burden of student debt for those who continue to higher education and also, as in Eastern Europe, the persistently unfavourable conditions in the housing market, effectively delay the process of transition still further. As a result, it is possible that many young people may no longer be able to 'grow up' at all. They are not just 'lost in transition', the notion of 'transition' itself may be lost, certainly as it is conventionally conceived in policy terms from dependence to independence.

As well as examining the economics of youth, particularly the rising costs of being a student, the chapter focuses on the general social and political consequences of young people's increased dependency on carers/ parents and the effect this is having on families. It also argues that the chances of making a 'successful transition' – if this is possible for the majority of the new genera- tion – continue to be affected by inequalities of (dis)ability, gender, ethnicity/ culture and, most saliently, class. Albeit that social class has undergone extensive transformation in the period we have reviewed so far and will continue to change in the future, it is influenced significantly if not decisively by the changes in educa- tion and training that we have also surveyed. In this respect, much of our attention is focussed on students. In the post-war period students as a whole formed a distinct minority group who were often differentiated from non-students on class lines. At the start of the twentyfirst century the relationship between the two now nearly numerically equal groups of students and non-students is changing as is the variety of student experience (Ainley and Weyers 2008).

Googling up the evidence

Although we referred disparagingly in Chapter 2 to 'research reduced to googling', such is the speed of social change – especially since the Credit Crunch in 2008 – that academic social research cannot keep up with it. This is not helped by the fact that academic research involves a long process of bidding for funding (very often unsuccessfully – initially at least), then of implementing and writ- ing up. By the time it appears – in journals that also take months at best to review and publish the material – findings are often of only historical interest.

There are also problems involved in surveying students across HE institutions that guard their reputations against others so that official approaches are often stymied. In this respect Student Unions (SUs) are useful entry points and the National Union of Students (NUS) is a source of invaluable data since it has direct access to its members – incidentally in what is the country's largest 'trade

union', if being a student is regarded as 'a trade'. (NUS is not affiliated to the Trades Union Congress.) SU surveys are often quickly
turned around and presented accessibly for a wide audience.

Private polling and marketing agencies are also interested in
the – for them – valuable custom of students and, while caution
should be taken with surveys that veer into product endorsement,
those who pay for such information require it to be accurate. The
two million-plus total number of full and part-time students above
A-level equivalent, including half a million post-grads (nearly one
quarter of all students 25+, 15 per cent from overseas including
8 per cent from the EU) in 165 Higher Education Institutions in
the UK (HEFCE 2009) make a huge market. Matthew Cheeseman
(2009) notes how they are serviced by 'an entrenched oppositional
entertainment industry selling [mainly] alcohol via the insistent
charm of youth culture'. Thus we draw below upon banks, estate
agents and even a pizza delivery company to access the current
situation, as well as upon newspaper reports, government statistics
and academic sources.

We also write from the personal experience of teaching in sixth
form and HE and as parents. And, as any parent will attest, providing for children in their late teens has become an increasingly
expensive undertaking, especially for students who have had the
most invested in them for longest. According to a survey by the
accountancy trade body, the Association of Accounting Technicans
(AAT) (www.aat.org.uk) relying on the Office of National Statistics
(ONS), in 1975 the average annual cost of a teenager was £700.
This compares with today's average teenager who needs up to
£9,000 per annum merely to 'get by' – not including 'necessities' like driving lessons. The survey lists and costs the extensive
number of electronic gadgets that now appear in a modern teen's
budget. Even though some of the 'essentials', like a hi-fi may have
been more expensive in 1975, items once considered 'luxuries',
like mobile phones, iPods, DVDs and Nintendo games consoles,
have, the ATT suggests, now become 'social necessities'. The
survey predicts that today's teenagers are facing a 'perfect storm'
as their increasingly expensive lifestyles coincide with recession,
growing youth unemployment, but also the decreased spending
power of their parents.

Students and the bank of mum and dad

According to a Royal Bank of Scotland (RBS)/ YouGov survey (http://www.rbs.com/media/news/press-releases/2008-press-releases/2008–11–20living-on-pocket-mon.ashx) today's UK teens receive an average of around £51 per month from parents. Even though these payments come with strings attached, in that 60 per cent of parents expect their children to pay their own travel fares, with a further 10 per cent insisting that school uniforms are covered and 20 per cent expecting this extra money to pay also the cost of essential study items and stationery. According to *The Telegraph* (4 February 2009) (www.telegraph.co.uk/family/4514445/Childrens-allowances-Money-tips-for-little-pockets.html), over the past decade pocket money has risen at 'gravity-defying rates' – with an average rise of 600 per cent for older children. In today's economic climate, children's allowances are the latest expenditure item being reviewed but *The Telegraph* reports many parents still fork out an average £381.52 per year paying bills for mobile phones and iPod music downloads on top of their children's normal allowances. According to the same paper (16 February 2006), only a third of parents expect their children to be able to manage alone financially after 18.

A YouGov survey reported in *The Guardian* (5 September 2008) found over 94 per cent of parents claiming to contribute financially towards their children after 18, while less than a third of their children said they had received help from their parents! According to this survey, commissioned by the insurance group Liverpool Victoria (http://www.lv.com), parents spend an average cumulative figure of £21,540 on supporting a child of 18+. Again, this is not counting day-to-day living expenses such as food and board but includes £6,735 towards the cost of university and other courses. Additional items comprised £5,600 towards buying a home, with nearly a third of the 1,200 parents surveyed contributing more than £9,000. The LV put the total cost of raising a child from birth to the age of 21 at £186,032, equivalent to £8,859 a year, £738 a month or £24.30 a day. It put the cost for children between years 12 to 18 at £43,992 (£6,285 p.a.), while for those supporting their children up to 21 the cumulative total increased substantially – up £36,746 (or £12,249 p.a.).

Increased costs to 18+ are compounded by the cost of being a student. According to RBS's annual Nat West Student Living Index for 2008, British students were likely to spend over £10.8 billion in housing and living costs over the academic year. Of this approximately £3.9 billion goes on rent, £1.2 billion on supermarket food shopping, £864 million on going out, £489 million on books and course materials and £773 million on cigarettes (a significant drop from 2007 when the smoking ban came in and students spent £806 million on cigarettes). The NatWest Index for 2009 (www. natwest.com/global/media/y2009/m-5.ashx) lists Birmingham as the cheapest student city in which to live at £171.14 per week with Oxford the most expensive at £238.38. According to *The Observer* (19 August 2007) in terms of rent alone, students in London were typically paying £102 per week.

According to the government's own Student Income and Expenditure Survey for 2007/08 (DIUS 2009), the average (mean) total expenditure of full-time English-domiciled students in 2007/08 was £12,254. Living costs constituted the largest category of spending for students, averaging £6,496 for full-time students (amounting to 53 per cent of their spending). Hardly surprising also are reports that the newly traditional gap year has fallen out of fashion as students realise the increased cost of study means that they or their parents can no longer afford a year abroad (*Guardian* 11 May 2009). Instead, some take gap years on graduation, working and travelling for lack of other alternative. On the other hand, students from poorer families may opt for a very different preliminary gap year in employment – if they can find it – while living at home as a way of saving money to finance university at home or away. Unavailability of such work contributed to the surge in demand for HE places in 2009.

The abolition of mandatory grants but also the imposition of tuition fees has further implications for the bank of mum and dad. Indeed, the Royal Bank of Scotland's 2006 'Financial Realism Survey' (http://www.rbs.com/media/news/press-releases/2006-press-releases/2006-06-012006-school-leavers-.ashx) reveals that during their first year at university, students graduating in 2006 expected to receive £442 million total financial support from their parents. This equated to an average of £773 per student during the academic year 2006–2007 (or £258 per term). According to RBS, a quarter of sixth-formers envisaged their parents would provide monthly contributions once they started university, whilst one in five were certain their parents would offer them *ad hoc* financial support if they needed it.

The survey showed that more than a third of sixth-formers (39 per cent) expected their parents to set up a regular standing order to their account – even if just one per cent expected their parents to pick up their term-time credit card bill! According to RBS, almost a third of sixth-formers (31 per cent) said they had not yet given any thought to university finances because they were preoccupied with studying. A further 28 per cent admitting to being worried about how they would manage for money at university. The RBS research indicated that the average UK sixth-former continued to underestimate the amount they would spend on various activities. For example, sixth-formers estimated an average of £186.30 per term on alcohol, whilst undergraduates actually spend an average of £274 each term. Sixth-formers also underestimate the amount they will spend on clothes by £27.50 per term and the amount they will spend on telephone and mobile phone bills by £15.60 each term.

Government information to parents makes it quite clear that parental contributions are expected from those families whose incomes are above levels which would qualify for maintenance grants of up to just under £3,000 per year:

> If you're the parent or partner of a student, you may be expected to make a contribution towards their living costs while they're at university or college . . . if you don't contribute, the student is unlikely to have enough money to fund their studies. (http://www.direct.gov.uk/en/EducationAndLearning/UniversityAndHigherEducation/StudentFinance/Parentsandpartners/DG_171587)

Many students will confirm that these contributions are not always forthcoming. Nevertheless, the Nat West index shows parents contributing £69.51 of students' weekly term time income, compared with £64.12 in 2008. According to the government's

Student Income and Expenditure Survey referred to above, on average, income from 'family and friends' represented 20 per cent of student total income (DIUS 2009: 17). There are of course differences. Students from routine/ manual backgrounds received substantially less in contributions from family and friends: at an average of £1,249, this comprised just 11 per cent of their total average annual income. This compared with 25 per cent of income for students with professional/ managerial parents who averaged £2,678.

The Telegraph reported (26 January 2008) that, like the Blairs for their son in Bristol:

> Many Britons are buying flats so their children can remain solvent during university, and as an investment. "Handout homes" – where a property is bought by one person for the use of another – are an increasingly common trend. There are now 327,000 handout homes in Britain, with a quarter bought by parents to house their children while they are studying. (www.telegraph.co.uk/ news/uknews/1576609/Parents-buy-for-children-2m-UK-second-homes.html).

This 'university effect' on the then buoyant buy-to-let housing market, which had grown by 26 per cent since 2000, was expected to continue with as many as 100,000 student-occupied second homes predicted by 2010.

This is not a new phenomenon and nor is the often commented on 'studentification' of certain towns, districts and areas of employment – for instance the bars and cafes around the universities in Manchester with their huge concentration of students. One of the authors, researching *Young People Leaving Home* in the 1980s, found at Edinburgh University two types of students – student landlords and student tenants, the former largely English and the latter Scots (Ainley 1991: 34). Indeed, Nicholson and Wasoff predicted 'a social division of students' there in 1989:

> On the one hand there will be those students (or their parents) who possess the financial capacity to enter owner occupation for the duration of their degree course, while on the other, those

who through necessity seek accommodation in the private rented sector. The outcome of this scenario will be that "student owner occupiers" leave university with a substantial capital asset and a significant advantage in their future housing prospects, while "student tenants" leave university to begin their professional and housing careers with a substantial debt to repay. (99–100)

Earning to learn and learning to earn

The fact that parents who are able continue to provide for their grown children while they are still learning should not disguise the fact that many parents cannot afford to do this, or not to any substantial extent. As a result, large numbers of the new generation of students slave away at Mcjobs to get by. According to a Learning and Skills Council survey reported by the BBC (www.news.bbc.co.uk: 14 November 2006), 40 per cent of teenagers in full-time learning had part-time employment with 28.2 per cent of 16 year olds working part-time during the same year. The government's Student Income and Expenditure Survey showed that in 2007/08 income from employment made up 20 per cent of income for full-time undergraduates. This equalled £2,108 on average and made income from paid work the joint second most important category of income for full-time students, along with family contributions. It also showed that 53 per cent of full-time students undertook some form of paid work during the academic year with average term-time earnings of £4,005. Overall, two-fifths of full-time students had a continuous/ permanent job in the 2007/08 academic year, while one-fifth had a non-continuous/ casual job. For the 40 per cent of full-time students who worked in continuous/ permanent jobs, the overall average number of hours worked across the academic year was 15 hours per week. This equated to around £100 per week on an average pay of £6.77 per hour.

However, not all students worked the same number of hours during term-time and vacations. Over two thirds (69 per cent) of full-time students who had a continuous job said that they worked different hours during term times and vacations: these students tended to work much longer hours during vacations (25 hours per week on average) than they did during term time (11 hours per week). The remaining 31 per cent of students who had continuous jobs averaged a steady 17 hours during term-time and vacation periods alike worked into the compressed cycles of their three term three years.

Research from the Halifax Bank (www.hbosplc.com/media) in 2008 showed that 60 per cent of students had a job (over a quarter of these having two) with 41 per cent of students in the survey working during term time. Almost a fifth of the students surveyed earned £50 to £100 per week, although in London 17 per cent earned more than £100. According to the Halifax, students in Scotland and Northern Ireland were the most likely to work the longest – with 23 per cent and 14 per cent respectively working 16–20 hours per week with only 8 per cent of London students in this category, while the average amount of working was between 8–9 hours per week. The Nat West statistics show Glasgow having the most students who work part-time (60 per cent) working 17.15 hours in their part-time jobs. Newcastle has the fewest students in work at 22 per cent. Out of 20 university towns, Brighton students have the highest weekly earnings, their weekly average of £128.29 offsetting much of their weekly £220.38 living expenses. Brighton students put in over 20 hours a week compared with the national average of 14 hours.

We have already noted the vicious circle in which students can become trapped working way beyond the ten hours per week recommended as a maximum to Scots students by the Cubie Report on student finance (Independent Committee 2000). Trying to escape, as one sixth former put it to one of the authors, 'a job where I don't have to stand up all day', they may end up in such a job either because they have not studied enough to pass the 2.1 hurdle that is equivalent to GCSE A*-C at this level, or because many retail jobs, even those where you have to stand up all day, are becoming graduatised. Many graduates therefore remain full-time in the jobs they undertook part-time as students. But as well as the question 'what was the point of study?', this also poses the question for students of when do they stop working to enjoy 'free time'? Also, in terms of what Lave and McDermott in Chapter 3 called 'alienated learning', who their 'work' of different types (study, employment, housework etc.) is for: themselves, their employer or their teachers?

A mountain of debt

Though parental contributions and part-time working play their part, the most common method of financing studies is by stacking up debt. The parallels with the larger economy need hardly be drawn! The abolition of mandatory grants was replaced by a student loan system in which 'mortgage style' repayment was to be deferred until labour market entry and an income of over £15,000. 'Upfront' tuition fees were abolished in 2007/08, but students would have to payback new 'variable' fees of up to £3,000. They also pay more for retakes and extra years, adding a further incentive to pass at all costs. The government's latest Student Income and Expenditure Survey shows loans and means-tested grants to be the main form of income for 46 per cent of full-time students – 84 per cent of full-time students received at least some income from loans and maintenance grants.

An MPs' briefing for 2007/08 showed that 88 per cent of students were accessing student loans, 41 per cent had bank overdrafts and 16 per cent were using commercial credit (www. parliament.uk/commons). Among those with student loans, the average debt was £9,100. For those using commercial credit the figure was £2,700. The average student bank overdraft was £1,000. Students from routine/ manual socio-economic backgrounds had higher levels of total borrowing (£9,400) than those from the professional and managerial classes (£8,700). They also had higher levels of commercial debt. Quoting NatWest data, the briefing put average graduate debt at just under £12,500 in 2007, up from £3,000 in 2000. These figures did not include those liable for 'variable fees'. Allowing for these, the briefing reported debt estimates of between £16,000 and £21,500 for students starting in 2008.

More recently still (2008/09), a survey by the student website *Push.co.uk* revealed that students who started at university in 2008 can expect to owe nearly £21,200 by the time they graduate and new students should reckon on at least £2,000 more than that.

This would then equal the current average graduate starting salary of £23,000 anticipated by the Association of Graduate Recruiters.

New types of student

According to data from the Social Issues Research Centre (SIRC) (2009), 33 per cent of student respondents claimed they could not afford university without living with their parents during term. The increased cost of being a student had resulted in 85 per cent considering living at home during university. Of people planning to start university for the first time, 27 per cent were intending to remain at home with 62 per cent of these admitting that a lack of money was the only reason keeping them at home while studying. Even Cambridge International Exams, commenting on UCAS data for 2009 applications observed:

> With one eye on fees, sixth-formers are looking at universities within commuting distance to save money, however around 65 per cent of those questioned felt that it was "completely fair" or "quite fair" that students should pay university fees. To save money, 68 per cent are looking at universities close to home, including 44 per cent who said they are only looking at universities within commuting distance. (www.cie.org.uk/news/pressreleases/detail?pressrelease_id=27729)

If the above observations are put in the context of the recession, they confirm a more general trend towards the emergence of 'new kinds of students' (Allen 2004) and the divisions Ainley and Canaan (2005) noted in the student experience between those living at home and those living away. Figures from the Higher Education Statistics Agency showed a 40 per cent increase in the number of students living with their parents between 1997 and 1999, immediately after the introduction of tuition fees. While a 2001 MORI survey reported in *The Times Higher* (19 January 2001) showed 21 per cent of respondents living with parents or family. This must be a much higher proportion today, certainly far from the traditional post-war conception of higher education as a liminal rite of passage before adulthood and independence/ home and living away. Instead, extended youth are unable to grow up even as they age.

For an increasing number, being a university student represents a continuation of – rather than a break from – existing routines. As we have seen, from a sample of students in a large Inner London sixth form (Allen 2004), it was clear that almost all expected to remain at home when they entered nearby universities and many hoped that they would be able to continue in the same part-time jobs that they had been doing while in the sixth-form. For these students going to higher education, although something they had aspired to, did not represent a fundamental change in lifestyle or a change in relationship with their families. For others who can afford it, 'going away to uni' may represent a (package) holiday-like, once-in-a-lifetime experience into which to cram as much as possible before returning to grim normality.

New types of parent

The SIRC data above confirms many young people today increasingly expect their parents to support them financially past the age of 18. They feel that it is, in a sense, the parents 'duty' to help them with going to university, getting married or, eventually, getting their own home. For this reason it seems that sentiments of dependency or even gratitude are not necessarily appropriate (SIRC: 11). With few respondents having any real sense of any obligation to repay parents for financial support given for university, rent or recurring costs, the report indicates that many young people also have an illusory sense of being at least 'partially' financially independent. Only a third of respondents felt being financially independent precluded them from receiving 'occasional support from parents' (13).

For some commentators, this new prolonged dependency is as much the consequence of a change in parental attitudes, as it is of the economic changes that have engulfed youth. Many parents now voluntarily take on responsibilities towards their offspring, or have the sort of presence in their children's lives that would have been considered inconceivable, or even inappropriate, in the past. Writing about university open days for example, Frank Furedi (2001) observed that 'not so long ago, many university students would have been embarrassed to be seen in the company of their mother and father' but it is now so common for this to happen that several universities make arrangements to accommodate them. According to Furedi, the idea of 'lifelong learning' encourages people to regard themselves as permanent students but it also reflects new 'cultural norms'. These call into question the idea of distinct developmental stages so that there is no clear line dividing the youthful learner from the intellectually self-sufficient mature adult. 'Overparenting', he argues, has led to 'paranoid parenting' and the creation of a generation of Peter Pan adults who 'never quite grow up'. It is not just a case of adult children needing their parents more. According to Furedi, twentyfirst century parents seem to have developed new needs and insecurities about their adult children.

In the opinion of the Head of Careers at Liverpool University, Dr Paul Redmond:

> It's a generational thing, Generation Y – those born from the 1980s onwards – have a completely different relationship with their parents from Generation X – those born in between the mid-1960s and the 1980s. Generation X would have been appalled at the idea. (*Guardian* 2 January 2008)

He described the influence of a new generation of 'helicopter parents', defined by the online encyclopaedia Wikipedia as 'a colloquial, early twentyfirst century term for a parent who pays extremely close attention to his or her child's or children's experiences and problems, particularly at educational institutions'. Redmond told BBC News (www.news.bbc.co.uk 4 January 2009) that helicopter parenting had now extended to intervening in post-university employment recruitment processes and 'some are even negotiating pay rises for them – it's like having a footballer's agent'!

This new level of parental involvement is both pragmatic and strategic. As status divisions within higher education become more marked, following the academic selection through largely literary examination of cultural capital as proxy for economic capital that we have remarked, helicopter parenting is a further extension of class power. It takes forward the 'pushy middleclass parent' syndrome that teachers have long had to deal with in schools. For previous generations, winning a place at university was considered an end in itself and almost guaranteed entry to a professional or managerial position. In a period of mass participation in higher education, the stakes for selecting the 'right' university are much higher. Just as they chose schools – and perhaps more importantly because they are continuing to pay for the education of their offspring – those parents who can afford to continue to protect their investments.

'Helicoptering' may be a new type of parenting for a minority but for increasingly large numbers of parents, lack of economic and cultural/ social resources means that the chance of being able to 'place' their children is minimal if non-existent. (See Pugsley 2004; also Reay et al. 2004.) This is exacerbated by the class-linked frequency of divorce, not only generally across society but particularly the tendency that Pugsley noted for middleclass parents to separate after their children left home for university. Simultaneously, parents may be looking after their own parents who may also move into a 'granny flat' in the home. The combination of all these and other factors is that, rather than benefiting from the equal opportunities of an open and socially mobile society, the reality for most young people and their parents who support them is exactly the opposite.

Students and students and non-students

Student experience varied so much in French universities even in 1964 that Bourdieu and Passeron (1979: 12–13) claimed students shared only:

> . . . the common feature that they study, that is, that, even in the absence of attendance or exercises, they undergo and experience the subordination of their occupational future to an institution

117

which, by means of the diploma, monopolizes an essential means of social success.

Contrariwise, Jary (2007: 96) suggested that 'the fundamental unity of the UK higher education system remains intact' with 'a remarkably cohesive academic culture' across UK HE. This supports Roberts' 2006 contention that an 'ideal student experience' is still shared as a social norm by all students. Lecturer Erik Ringmar was dismissed from the London School of Economics (LSE) in the same year for advising applicants that the teaching there was no better than at a former-polytechnic – in fact, worse because teaching was done by post-graduates since LSE lecturers were too busy researching to teach. He argued that:

> the in-class experience of an LSE student differs very little from the in-class experience of any other university' because 'University courses are pretty much the same wherever you go' but 'where the LSE really stands out [is] its student body [which] makes it vastly different from other universities, not just in the UK but in the world. (*Times Higher* 18 August 2006)

The point is not what students are taught but what they learn. Since Ainley (1994: 120) showed 'staff and students collude in consolidating institutional identities which are socially distinctive', it can be asserted that it is the social constitution of the student body at different institutions that determines what students learn. This also explains how their qualifications are ranked subsequently by employers (for which see Brown et al. 2004).

Roberts' notion of a persisting normative ideal of the student experience rests on the contrast of all students with all non-students. Even though he has also drawn attention to the fact that, with many more people in higher education, students become more like the rest of the population, their predominant norms include binge drinking and some sexual experimentation besides other expectations that are shared with many non-students. Still Roberts persists in maintaining that students can be differentiated from non-students and therefore widening participation has merely widened the constitution of the new middle-working class (2009). Despite the deepening indebtedness it entails for most, Roberts maintains that this difference and the difference in employment prospects for graduates compared with non-graduates sustains the demand for higher education.

Is this characterisation still appropriate given the new economic situation? Not all non-students can be consigned to a new 'under-class', which would be the obverse of this argument. Nor are all students the same in a more differentiated HE system. Rather, many students are more similar to non-students than they are to others in the student body. The 'business as usual' lifestyle of the London sixth form students has been referred to above, but with the reversal of the gender polarities in HE, there is now a considerable overlap between the majority of 'home based' young women (overrepresented, as we noted in the last chapter, in the lower tiers of mass HE) and their boyfriends, many of whom are not students. If fees were waived for locally living students, the division between students living at home or living away might become at least as important as the division between students and non-students, especially if – mediated by television series such as *Hollyoaks* – it is believed to be different.

Though there are some exceptions – for instance, many Muslim parents wanting their children to study from home, particularly if they are female – as we have argued, the decision to move away is strongly influenced by ability to pay – in other words by class. The likely increase in part-time learning with full-time working and online students might, we suggested in Chapter 3, help the govern-ment meet its 50 per cent target, along with linking some of the new apprenticeships with Foundation 'degrees' awarded by local universities but franchised to FE colleges. This can only entrench the salience of this new division amongst and between students and their institutions still further, adding to the snobbery, racism and sexism that raddles the hierarchy of competing universities and colleges from top to bottom.

Anecdotally, the folklorist Matthew Cheeseman (referred to above) records rival groups of Sheffield and Hallam students taunt-ing one another with adapted football chants. While graffiti in a Greenwich University urinal attests to similar hostility between non-students and students with 'Go and get a job you student ponces', scrawled in one hand followed by 'Like I should care what a bog-cleaner thinks!' scribbled in response in another. At the top of the tree meanwhile, a student told Ainley and Weyers (2008: 145), 'Oxford [is] definitely upper middleclass. Some are hugely rich'. Adding, 'I used to think I was middleclass until I went to Oxford!'

A place of your own?

Despite the differences between them, the situation of young people in general has been worsened by the housing crisis. As proposed in Chapter 1, in the post-war period, the process of leaving home was just part of a more general transition to adulthood, often being a consequence of marriage. In the light of the uncertainties of today, the post-war transition to adulthood can be idealised as 'unproblematic'. For example, the actual process of leaving is in danger of being underplayed when it has always been an extremely significant event. 'Home' as Jones (1995: 93) reminds us, is the 'locus of inequality between parents and children'. Even if young people may refer to it as 'theirs' and it is the place that, as American poet Robert Frost wrote, 'when you have to go there, They have to take you in', home is, or at least has been, essentially a parental home. Legally, young people over 18 (16 in Scotland) remaining in their parents' or guardians' home beyond the age of 18, live in it as 'licensees' – in other words, with the permission of their parents.

In the post-war period and particularly in the years that followed, young people often experienced a period of 'transitional' housing – many amongst the working class living with relatives or with in-laws. By contrast, if they did not return home for a short time, middleclass youth were more likely to share intermediate or post-university accommodation with friends (Jones 1995: 27). If 'transitional housing' was a regular feature in young people's lives, Jones also argues that – even if some parents regarded their children leaving as something 'final' – many young people left home 'temporarily', taking with them parental assurances that they would always be welcomed back 'if it didn't work out'

(Jones 1995: 73). Even if returning home may have been seen as a regression by the young people concerned and sometimes by their parents, transition was not always final and one way.

In many cases, Jones reminds us, leaving home could and can still be an emotionally fraught process: the consequence of a row with parents or other family members, for example. Describing the situation in the early 1990s, Jones reports that even if one third had then left home by the age of 19, 28 per cent of those were to return at one stage or another. Financial reasons have always been near the top in any list of reasons young people give for either not leaving or returning to their parents' home (Ainley 1991). Many young people have always depended on support from their parents in setting up home, even if the nature of this support as well as the amount, invariably depended on parents' economic status and may have involved a process of 'complex negotiation' (Jones 1995: 101).

In the past, youth 'homelessness' was associated with poverty and seen as a problem of the 'few', even after it became relatively common on Britain's streets from the 1980s on. Although its significance should not be underplayed (Mizen 2004: 116), today many are caught between the two poles of being neither rich enough to buy nor poor enough to qualify for public housing, so that 'homelessness' has become equated with living in somebody else's home. This situation has been exacerbated in that it arises just when 'home ownership' has come to be considered something that everybody should aspire to. As with education and employment, it is those whose parents would be considered to be somewhere in the 'middle' who have been encouraged to be the most aspirational – to dream of buying a home of their own. As with education and employment also, it is likely that this group, who were expected to enjoy even greater consumer choice than their parents ever did, will be the most disappointed.

By the end of 2007, as what had become the housing 'bubble' burst, Halifax, the UK's largest lender and part of the HBOS group, reported that first-time buyers had been effectively priced out of the market in 96 per cent of towns in Britain (*Guardian* 22 December 2007) while in the prosperous south-east, prices were ten times the average local income. A key determinant of the ability to purchase a property is the ratio of mortgage payments against income. In the last quarter of 2007, mortgage interest payments made up 20 per cent of income with the average advance being £11,845 on an income (combined or otherwise) of just over £35,549. This represents an income multiple of 3.39 (Council of Mortgage Lenders 2008) and the average age 29–31 (effectively the assumption of adulthood, coincident with the rising age of first marriage age or at least childbirth for the property-owning 'new middle working' class). This was an increase from 11.8 per cent of income and a multiple of 2.83 in 2005. Though interest payments had been higher in the past (27 per cent in 1990), this largely resulted from a period of rocketing interest rates (reaching 12 per cent in 1994). Income multiples remained approximately the same at 2.31.

Whatever happened to public housing?

There is not the space, nor is it the focus of this book on education, to provide a detailed account of the changing economics of housing. However, we have said enough already to show that housing is an essential background to understanding the current situation of the younger generation and that the growing cost of accommodation has continued to impede the ability of young people to gain meaningful independence. The cost of housing at the start of the twentyfirst century now means, we would argue, that for many young people 'leaving home' is simply impossible.

Of course, house prices were hiked up as part of the 'asset inflation' that drove Blair's consumer boom, creating a situation where at the height of the bubble 70 per cent of London properties were being bought for investment. Yet, as Toby Lloyd from the think-tank *Compass* shows, there has also been a huge contraction in private-sector house-building with the number of housing starts half those of 1988 and less than a third compared with the 350,000 in 1968 (Lloyd 2009). Particularly significant has been the decline in public housing.

In their historic Bethnal Green study, Wilmott and Young described an area where two borough councils owned more than a third of the residences. In the 1950s, Local Authorities built as many as 250,000 units a year – from tower blocks to cottage-style brick terraces. In comparison, during the twentyfirst century as few as 130 council houses have been built each year, while five million people will be on the waiting list for social housing by 2012 (*Guardian* 6 July 2009). Much of the decline has been the consequence of the 'Right to buy' policy introduced by Mrs Thatcher (Hanley 2008). Since 1989, councils have had to give back to the Treasury at least 75 per cent of the income they receive in rents and sales for their remaining stock. As a consequence, much of any new social housing has been provided by housing associations: there were only 22,000 new starts in 2007/08 – local councils starting just 680 (Lloyd 2009).

Public housing has not only decreased in availability but where it does exist has become re-categorised as 'social housing', designed for a needy minority without any necessary long term connection to an area. Dench, Gavron and Young (2006: 47) refer to the 'ladder principle' used in East London housing where local housing was allocated to the most 'deserving' – loyal tenants of long standing who were also often 'bastions of the community' waiting patiently for flats on the most desired estates. Dench et al. go on to describe the negative effects of the changes in the way social housing is now allocated following new principles of individual need on the attitude, politics and collectivism of established working-class communities.

There have also been negative changes in the private rented sector. While, according to Wilmott and Young at least, the preferential allocation of council housing to children of existing tenants was strictly forbidden, private landlords continued to adopt a 'sons and daughters' principle, whereby existing tenants either secured new tenancies for family members through 'speaking to the rent man' (1961: 47) or passed on their own tenancies. It is likely that similar forms of collective property rights existed in other localities but changes in the practice and the legalities of private renting led to a steady increase in rents. By July 2009, despite an apparent fall in average rents with the collapse of the 'buy to let' market as owners unable to sell their properties resorted to renting, the average monthly rent for a one bedroom property was still listed as £392-£795, in London £795. (www.rentright.co.uk)

The consequences of these developments for young people are clear. In April 2009 *Social Trends*, published by the Office for National Statistics, reported that a third of men and a fifth of women aged between 20 and 34 still lived with their parents. For the 20–24 age group, the Social Issues Research Centre (2009) put the figure at almost 60 per cent for men and 40 per cent of women. A few months later, newspapers were carrying the results of survey commissioned by Giovanni Rana Fresh Pasta (!), which found one in three men aged between 20 and 40 were still living with their parents (Tuesday 2009). This compared with one in five women of the same age. The study of 3,000 men and women revealed that almost a quarter (24 per cent) still lived at home with their parents. Cost was the main factor for 59 per cent of them. According to *Social Trends*, around four in ten people in the UK aged 15–30 said the main reason for remaining at home was that they couldn't afford to move out, 44 per cent identifying lack of affordable housing. Almost seven out of ten would-be first time buyers (we can assume the majority can be characterised as being 'young') were reported to have given up hope of ever owning a home (*Guardian* 25 May 2009).

Rethinking 'transition' and social class

It is clear that young people considered to be a 'new middle' in society face the greatest contradictions. This generation of over-qualified but now underemployed youth may end up being poorer than the parents who have invested in their future aspirations. Indeed, Andy Green (2009) indicates a shift in wealth to older generations, predicting intergenerational conflict as a result. This is reflected in the labour market changes described in Chapter 1 with the disappearance of 'youth' jobs but also in recent Labour Force Survey figures (*Guardian* 17 September 2009) which, while recording shocking unemployment figures for those under 25, also show large numbers of people of retirement age still working. Smart (1997) indicated how changes in the family (from extended to nuclear to serial family structures) are also affecting access to parental support. This underlines the danger of basing policy on outmoded models, for instance devising tax policies to shore up the monogamous nuclear family. Though this book is concerned primarily with England, the longer term consequences of 'delayed adulthood' (Cote and Bynner's 'emergent adults' in Canada and Europe, Roberts' *Youth in Transition* in Eastern Europe) have already become visible elsewhere. In 1973 only 6 per cent of recent university leavers in France were unemployed whereas now the rate is between 25 and 30 per cent as at the same time property prices have doubled or trebled. Whereas in 1970 salaries for 50 year olds were only 15 per cent higher than for those who were 30, the gap is now 40 per cent. Similar developments are reported in Spain, Italy and Germany (Keeley, Burke and Kington 2008).

As another example of what Gill Jones (2009: 110) calls the 'mismatch between policy models of youth and the reality of young people's lives', so that 'Policies are still based on normative standardized biographies' and 'The linearity of policy models of youth lead to a continuing dependence on age-structuring in legislation', there has never been any specific public housing provision for young people – save recently perhaps with foyers for homeless youngsters. Yet, 'Through a policy of reductionism, age – as a policy-driven construct – is becoming more significant just at a time when culturally it should be becoming less so' (121). In particular, there is 'a critical threshold developing at 18 or 19 years old' (111). Jones rejects the dependence to independence paradigm in favour of a recognition of interdependence. Nevertheless, Ken Roberts points out that 'most young adults [in East and West Europe] still achieve and settle, in careers or jobs that will support an adult lifestyle, the majority will still form nuclear families . . .' (2009: 118). He therefore wants to retain the concept of 'transition' but will the changes we have described mean that it will continue to be useful in future?

We follow Jones (and indeed Roberts) in maintaining, as we have said, that class differences remain most influential on the life course, along with – to a statistically less significant extent – those of ability, ethnicity and culture, gender and sexual orientation. It is paradoxical however that awareness of class has decreased even as its influence would appear to be decisive. We have argued that this

125

is because the class structure itself is also in a process of ongoing transformation, affected – as we have said – but not determined by changes in the education system. Old perceptions of traditional 'middle' and 'working' classness thus persist mixed up with new notions of class and also of classlessness. The application of new technology and the expansion of services has eroded the manual/ non-manual division which cut across the post-war class pyramid. In some ways the new education system with its old fashioned academic selection sought to recreate those halcyon grammar school days of social mobility. It also attempted to educate the working class out of existence, perhaps in the way the comprehensives might also have been intended to do by government. These popular memories of clearly defined middle and working classes are confused with the new Americanised notion of a middle-working/ working-middleclass defined against an 'underclass'. Again, the upper or ruling class is elided from this schematisation, even though – in both models – the notion of a 'middle' class only makes sense if it is in the middle between an upper class above and a lower class below – 'between the snobs and the yobs', as has been said. (See Ainley 1993 for a discussion.) As Roberts notes (2001: 169–192) the upper or ruling class, though constituted by less than 1 per cent of the whole population, is 'the smallest . . . best organised . . . and most class conscious class.'

These considerations relate to habitual sociological concerns and that staple of first year sociology seminars: whether higher education (any longer) makes you middleclass (if you weren't already). This discussion is often lost upon sociology students who share the reluctance, first noted by Bourdieu and Passeron in 1964, for students who are determinedly meritocratic and 'entirely occupied in choosing what they are to be' to 'generally evade the simple naming of their parents' occupation, whatever it may be' (1979: 38). As well as confusions between perceptions of the shifting nature of social class (above), there is also nowadays a type of political correctness that forbids open discussion of social class, as Ainley and Bailey noted amongst FE students in the 1990s:

> Even the Home Counties College A-level sociology students, despite covering the sociology of education in their syllabus,

though they asserted that everyone on whatever course at the College was "the same", could not explain how it happened that no one in the class actually knew, or was friends with, anyone doing hairdressing at the College, although one conceded, "It seems that lots of people who live on the estates in Market Town have gone on to do hairdressing". (1997: 79)

These 16–18 year olds students were more likely to accept gender if not ethnicity as a significant social determinant since, as the Students' Union President at the College put it, 'there aren't really things like if you're this class or this type of person you therefore do this course. Everybody's treated as an equal'. (ibid.)

This is of course the official ideology of the institutions and is widely accepted, along with the reiterated message of F&HE lecturers that 'It's up to you' how well you do in university or college, so that 'You only have yourself to blame' if you do not achieve. Moreover, people tend to compare themselves with those they know, not social groups which have become increasingly remote from them with accelerating social polarisation and the actual decrease in social mobility from the 1980s on. Hence, Roberts argues that 'higher education has become the first stage at which social class inequalities become glaring'. Up until then, 'given that for so many their futures are difficult to predict . . . young people with different class origins and destinations rub shoulders in the same schools'. Or at least, 'share the same leisure interests' (2009: 164). Thus Roberts explains the lack of even 'the mildest' class consciousness, if not of ethnic, national and other solidarities amongst his East European cohorts.

In the UK, this is debateable to say the least and depends on the awareness of class-linked schooling. As Jones says (2009: 178), 'Young people's class careers have been delayed with the extension of education, and so they remain under the influence of their class of origin for longer'. Certainly, as Roberts concedes, 'Those who succeed know they owe a great deal to their families . . . [and] are determined to do the same for their own children by paying for private education when this seems advisable' (163).

However, it is not simply the economic position of parents, but also the 'social' and 'cultural' advantages that young people are usually able to enjoy as a result – Bourdieu's 'cultural capital' for which academic qualifications are a proxy. Bourdieu also uses the term 'social capital' (Robbins 1991) to describe resources based on connections – who you or they know. In other words, parental ability to ensure their offspring get the 'best' education available, for example, and to ensure that they mix with people of similar social backgrounds to themselves, or are simply in the right place at the right time. Putnam (2000) calls this a form of 'bridging capital' (good), the possession of which allows one to either advance up the social structure, or more likely, to be able to maintain one's position within it; whereas 'bonding capital' (bad) holds you back under the influence of your peer group.

It could be argued therefore that the relatively smooth process of what we called 'collective transition' experienced by many working-class youth in the post-war years was essentially the result of a 'collective culture', not only shared in the workplace but in the community and family. Even if this did not promote mobility or movement up the social structure, it acted as a kind of 'bonding' in that it served as an unofficial system of social security as well as providing a sense of identity and order. Our argument is that with the breaking down of the traditional occupational divisions, many of these collective responses – what the Centre for Contemporary Cultural Studies, among others, referred to as an oppositional 'working-class culture' – have largely been replaced by a commercialised mass youth culture.

Like Roberts' East European youth, some young people welcome the end of old certainties, as one of the authors found interviewing the students referred to above in FE colleges in the 1990s: 'Rather than being sentenced to a secure job for life, this could be welcomed as quite an inviting prospect for a young and energetic person. Particularly, as learning and earning might also be interspersed with leisure and travel' (Ainley and Bailey 1997: 96). But while:

> many interviewees could welcome a move away from dependence upon work – especially the prospect of just one job for their whole life – until they reflected that, without parental or other support, they would require some other source of income to

sustain them in the periods between moving from one different job to another. Such a reflection gave pause to even the most confident and assured. While . . . to those who lacked the personal resources – material and educational – to entertain it, this prospect of enterprising and varied forms of contracted and self-employment did not appeal at all. They sought instead the security of "a steady job" in which they could "keep their heads down" and "hang on" if not "get on". (97)

The collapse of traditional cultures and structures of society has fostered attempts to reconceptualise the process of transition from youth to adulthood. Post-modern writers, like Giddens (1991) and Beck (1992), welcome the disappearance of many of the old certainties. While making life more insecure and 'individualised', this has also given rise to what Beck calls the 'forcible emancipation' of youth. It requires them to develop a variety of 'strategies' to navigate the twentyfirst century 'risk society'. Such writers do not reject the concept of a 'transition' from youth to adulthood, only the idea of any collective transition to pre-determined destinations. In other words, they imply that individual's 'reflexive biographies' are largely a product of their own actions. As their 'biographies' unfold, individuals not only reflect upon but also reassess where they are going and make changes. (See introduction to Ainley (ed.) 2008 for a discussion in relation to student writing which is proposed as a means to make students aware of the objective similarities of their subjective experiences. Also McLean and Abbas 2009.) An emphasis on individualism does not mean that young people cannot have the same experiences, just that it is impossible to predict the exact nature of these, or when they might happen. For example, it is argued that young people today make their transitions in roundabout ways returning to education after a period in the workplace, working but continuing with their studies part-time, or taking time out from studying to spend time travelling.

It is also important to distinguish between those who Jones (2009) refers to as being forced into 'short term' survival strategies and those able to make 'long term' plans. Short term survival strategies may end up being a series of *ad hoc* decisions made by those with limited social capital to draw on; in other words, with the least power to determine or to alter their circumstances. Those able to plan 'long term' tend to be from economically privileged groups. In this respect, the usefulness of incorporating the concept of 'strategies' into a new understanding of transition is extremely limited and, for growing sections of the population, unrealistic.

While it is important to re-establish the importance of action or 'agency' in the lives of young people and whilst recognising the richness and variety of individual experience, the notion of 'individualisation' will be challenged in the following chapter. It will suggest that young people have always had 'collective strategies' – courses of action that deliver results – and that they have mainly been pragmatic rather than idealistic in their aspirations. The question for their parents, teachers and others of the older generations working with them is how best to support young people in these practices in ways that are best for them in the short and long term, recognising that in the long term they are the ones who will live that future which gives the present its meaning.

5

New Directions for Youth and Education

Introduction

This book is primarily about what Phil Cohen (1997) called *the Youth Question* – how society integrates new generations to ensure its own reproduction. We have argued that in the 1980s education became the main economic policy of government; or rather, was substituted for the absence of any economic policy other than to follow the global 'free' market. As a result, institutionalised learning now occupies an increasing amount of time in the lives of young people for longer periods of time. It starts earlier and goes on longer – if it ever ends. New Labour's standards agenda, particularly the way in which it was organised around a business model of *Education plc*, was intended to improve the 'supply side' by raising the quality of human capital since, in the knowledge economy of the twentyfirst century, highly educated labour would supposedly always be at a premium. According to successive governments, the new knowledge economy allowed 'more room at the top' and globalised labour markets were supposed to provide boundless opportunities for those with high levels of qualifications or so-called 'skills'. Those without would struggle to survive. This ideological justification, which legitimated the intensification and expansion of education to influence so many people's lives – not just the pupils, students and trainees and their teachers who were most directly affected – has now collapsed.

A large section of this book has been devoted to detailing the failure of these policies. We have related how, though 'standards' – as expressed in terms of examination qualifications and SATs scores – have continued to rise, there have not been corresponding opportunities for moving up in the labour market. Even if the current generation of young people are, without question, the most highly qualified (or at least certified) ever, many increasingly find themselves 'overqualified and underemployed'. We have likened the situation facing many young people to walking up a down escalator where you have to run faster and faster simply to stay still. For example, even though participation in higher education has increased to 43.5 per cent of the cohort, only a small number, drawn mostly from the upper and upper middle sections of society, enter the more prestigious universities that any longer guarantee 'graduate jobs' (Williams and Filippakou 2009). At the other end of the scale, a largely uncertified – or worthlessly certified – so-called 'underclass' is socially excluded on the margins of society. Educational expansion has accompanied and reinforced social polarisation. In the middle, the oversupply of graduates has meant that, with a larger pool to choose from, lesser remunerated jobs are becoming graduatised, putting pressure on those who previously occupied such roles.

We have also discussed whether all or some of the new generation are increasingly 'lost in transition' because transitions themselves have become so uncertain – from education to employment, home to living away, or from dependence to 'independence'. In this sense it can be said that people are 'lost' as the media now refer to the younger generation in general. Certainly, compared to the period of genuine if limited social mobility during the post-war period, the minority who then experienced a 'prolonged' semi-dependency on their parents while they were 'away' at university or college were generally able to choose from a variety of careers. Many graduates today are not only socially but also geographically immobile – unable to find appropriate work, unable to pay off student debts and unable to afford to leave the family home.

Key to our analysis has been the argument that, rather than concentrating on developing the real intrinsic qualities of their students – stimulating curiosity to develop the self-confidence that young people need to change the world – the schools, colleges and universities that have come to play such a large part in young people's lives have become little more than what Stanley Aronowitz (2008) described in the USA as 'credential mills', churning out academically certificated students for employers to select those few they currently require and disappoint the rest. As a consequence, students at all levels of learning are alienated from learning and adopt a largely instrumental approach to their studies. They memorise particular pieces that are required and devote large amounts of time to improving their examination technique through the endless practice of past papers and the unquestioned construction of 'model answers'.

This chapter sets out some alternative principles through which learning could be organised, building on some of the themes that we provided elsewhere (Allen and Ainley 2007) and revising others. In it, we argue that, rather than experiencing a commodified or a 'reified' relationship with society because of their distorted economic dysfunction, schools, colleges and universities need to be reclaimed as a community resource. Education would then serve as a means of emancipation rather than as an instrument of social control. For example, education should allow people to develop what early nineteenth century radicals referred to as 'really useful knowledge'. Nowhere would this be more important than in the relationship between education and the economy.

Supply and demand: The economics of youth unemployment

The most pressing concern is the rising level of youth unemployment which will continue to increase well after the recession officially 'ends'. The collapse in recruitment of young people in more and more sectors of the economy has already left one in five – one in four, according to some estimates – of the 16–24 age group out of work and in danger of being classified as NEET. That is nearly one million of the two and a half million unemployed at the time of writing in August 2009. The government belatedly realised that everything cannot be 'left to education' and intervened more directly in the youth labour market. For example, in addition to existing work placement schemes and the programme-led apprenticeships, where – like YTS trainees before them – 'apprentices' receive an allowance rather than a proper wage, it encouraged employers to offer 'internships' where graduates work for nothing to gain the experience they lack. Doubtless it was hoped these would be temporary measures and, even though inequitable, that they would enhance the chances of young people when the labour market started to 'work' again. Of course, everybody concerned about the future of young people would not only welcome these opportunities if they were properly remunerated, but many would also call for them to be expanded.

Likewise, teacher unions, particularly the National Union of Teachers (NUT) and the Universities and College Union (UCU) are also correct in calling for greater expenditure on education to compensate for the effects of the recession, even if, in themselves, these measures are also merely a holding operation. More F&HE places would at least give more people the chance to 'drift up' instead of being 'squeezed out' of the system. Concentrating on the supply side of the market economy, they are a continuation of New Labour's drive to improve the education and skills of the workforce – in other words to make labour more 'employable'. This will never be enough however if there continues to be an overall shortage in the number of jobs available and a lack of demand for labour. Supply side measures, as we will argue, have to be accompanied by increased demand so that educational reform must go hand in hand with labour market reform and regulation. Nevertheless, creating enough university places for all young people who want them would constitute a short term measure to reduce unemployment.

As noted in Chapter 3, the 2009 budget also announced the creation of 'socially useful' jobs for young people under 25 who had been out of work for a year – subsequently reduced by Gordon Brown to ten months as his own future employment looked increasingly insecure (*Observer* 30 August 2009)! The 150,000 extra vacancies promised would either be in the public sector where Local Authorities were to be subsidised at £1,500 per head to take on 50,000 extra staff, or franchised out to private providers. The first of these new jobs were announced in July 2009 at a cost of £300 million. They included employment as classroom assistants, sports coaches and in care homes, as well as on projects to improve recycling and refurbish council housing. These opportunities were really 'elastoplast' solutions – likely, in many cases, to be no more than six month contracts at the national minimum wage. After that time they would predictably leave many young people back where they started a few months previously. Also, these measures only added to the number of low paid jobs in the service sector.

Despite these weaknesses, these moves represent a step in the right direction, albeit a small one. Rather than concentrating almost exclusively on 'supply-side' remedies – attempts to make young people more attractive to employers who have scaled down recruiting or even stopped completely, they represent at least a tacit admission that for the moment, because jobs do not exist they need to be created. As Paul Gregg and Richard Layard of the London School of Economics also show (www.cep.lse.ac.uk), the additional taxation revenue that would be generated means the cost of providing jobs is invariably less than the cost of keeping young people out of work for six months.

Longer term and more permanent solutions to youth unemployment will only be possible through the implementation of wider economic policies that restore general levels of demand in the economy but also allow a central role for an expanded public sector so as to ensure guaranteed employment rather than taking one's chance with failed market forces. In the absence of any concrete proposals, we would suggest the implementation of what 'old fashioned' socialists used to call a 'programme of public works' paid at the rate for the job to repair but also recreate sustainable local infrastructures, improve local services and housing. Supporting this could be a network of local youth employment boards and 'recruiting pools' where employer vacancies can be matched with young people's needs and where a Local Authority, for example, could – to borrow language from the financial sector – act as a 'lender of last resort' for those young people still without employment.

Until relatively recently, these sorts of policies would have sounded completely Utopian but recession and the Credit Crunch have brought the previously discredited ideas of public owner-ship and nationalisation back on the policy agenda. Questions about 'how we would pay for it?' have also been answered with policies that conventional economics had consigned to the waste bin as budget deficit spending, along with the importance of the Keynesian maxim that 'what somebody else spends somebody else will earn', have returned as part of the vocabulary of 'bust' economics.

Youth services, along with schools, colleges and universities, can anticipate severe cuts after the 2010 election. However, whichever Party wins faces a double-bind in its youth and welfare/ social security policies generally in that cuts to, for example, the infor-mal education of youth and community work will only produce greater expense to the state elsewhere – in police and prisons, etc. Similarly, reducing expenditure on post-compulsory education by raising fees (let alone attempting to raise additional charges from 'top-ups' to basic voucher entitlements for compulsory schooling raised to 17 and then 18) leaves no other option whilst there are no jobs except welfare to work schemes. Hence, there is no real alternative except for reflating a greened economy that is more labour – and learning – intensive than the part-time, insecure, low skill, low wage, service sector McJobs that for many are virtually all that are currently available. A green economy is also ecologi-cally imperative (Campaign against Climate Change 2009). As we have said, such ideas until recently appeared Utopian. Now Utopia is presented as necessary for human survival.

A new economic literacy

After governments on both sides of the Atlantic have subsidised the banks and other major financial institutions to prevent their collapse, it is temping to conclude that the dominance of the 'neoliberal' economic model – to which New Labour and the Tories before them proclaimed education the servant – is over (as Mason 2009). Unlike previous recessions when progressives, radicals and particularly socialists put the case for economic planning, job crea-tion and economic democracy – examples being Keynes himself in the 1930s but also Andrew Glyn's 1985 proposals for creating 'a million jobs a year' – there has not been a clear consensus about alternatives and few blueprints for what to do next and so the opportunity to put forward alternatives is being lost. Possibly, many on the political left, hoping the slump would finally lead to 'the end of capitalism', have been disorientated by government intervention into the banking system. So they have allowed discussion of how the increased level of public sector borrowing might propel a new emphasis on social justice to be superseded by one in which the central objective is to return to economic orthodoxy and reduce the size of the fiscal deficit. Yet this deficit is still not huge compared to that at the end of the Second World War, for example, and the proportion of national debt to national income is still lower than in many countries.

Similarly, focus on an unfair tax system which has facilitated ever greater economic inequality has been lost to the assumption that taxation as a whole should be increased to pay for the crisis. With military budgets under strain, there has been little mainstream debate about whether that money could be better spent than on rearming, trident and ID cards etc. Perhaps most importantly, as many have pointed out, even as it grows more pressing, the green agenda has been subordinated to restoring economic growth at all costs.

A consequence of the passive role that education has played in relation to these debates and others is the lack of any real critical awareness or organised opposition from the mass of the student population who in the 1960s were considered to be a vanguard of change. The biggest downturn for seventy-five years was received complacently by a population that is generally economically illiterate. It was even ignored by many teachers and lecturers in 'secure' public sector employment and under pressure to deliver 'learning targets,' but feeling powerless to raise controversial issues with their students. The lack of organised response from school-leavers and students is perhaps not surprising. If the failure to secure employment in line with one's aspirations is seen as failure on the part of the individual rather than as being part of a much wider social problem, the immediate response for many is to 'keep your head down' and accept that you have to return to education to gain more qualifications so as to improve your place in 'the queue'. Hence, the recent surge in demand for university places, not only from young people but also from unemployed adults.

A different education system would embody a different relationship between education and a sustainable economy. It would be an education system that was designed to promote collective responsibility and encourage community action rather than concentrating on individual advancement through obtaining the right qualifications. Using education to promote economic reconstruction and democracy would empower people to take an active part in a broader democratic discussion about the best policies for sustainability, economy and employment. Such an approach would represent an inversion of the 'master-servant' relationship of education to the economy we have described. A more reflexive relationship, interest in and discussion about the economy would go much further than simply seeking to meet existing economic performance indicators since the imperative of sustainability rules out the assumption of endless growth. The social legacy of the neoliberal phase also needs to be addressed, such as the implications of an increasingly polarised labour market, not to mention the devastating effects of mass youth unemployment.

Despite the steady erosion of young peoples' position in the labour market over the last thirty years and more since the collapse of apprenticeships, it is unlikely that any young person about to finish their education and look for work would have had any formal opportunity to appraise the issues involved. Despite government claims for the economic relevance of education, many young people rightly feel that what is taught in school, college and often at university has little relation to the issues they will have to address after they leave. Careers advice about employment from a privatised Careers Service occasionally contracted in to schools but no longer as a part of an entitlement to the Connexions Service (as was), invariably turns into advice about post-16 and HE decision-making, partly because these are the only remaining options.

Schools teach little about the economic realities of the world that young people will enter. During the early years of the National Curriculum 'Economic Awareness' was only one of a number of 'cross curricula' themes that had little status alongside the ten mandatory subjects. In the current version of the National Curriculum, at Key Stage 4 (14–16 year olds), economic awareness is invariably delivered through a 'work based learning entitlement' which may only involve the now customary 'work experience' and a variety of 'enterprise days', or through a non-statutory 'Education for economic wellbeing and financial capability'. According to the QCA (http://curriculum.qcda.gov.uk/key-stages-3-and-4/subjects/pshe), it 'aims to equip students with the knowledge, skills and attributes to make the most of changing opportunities in learning and work'(!). While, as we will argue, it is still possible for teachers to make good use of the critical space that this provides, these initiatives are often really no more than 'bolt-ons' – part of a largely *ad hoc* personal and social education programme mixed with 'Citizenship'. As most of it is not formally assessed or recorded in any league table it plays second fiddle to the examination roll out and sadly, in many cases, is not taken seriously by many students.

Of course, students have the option of choosing 'economics' as one of their examination courses at sixth-form, with many schools and colleges perhaps unsurprisingly reporting large increases in student interest in a subject that has, up until now, remained rather abstract if not 'elitist' (Stanford 2008) to many youngsters making their A-level choices. But, as mentioned earlier, with teachers under pressure to finish the syllabus and to prepare their students for examination questions which are prepared some time in advance, their flexibility to relate to current news stories, let alone any willingness to critique, is seriously compromised. As a result, in the summer of 2009 when 'boom' had turned to 'bust' and young people's employment prospects continued to decline, A-level economics candidates could still find themselves answering questions about the dangers of inflation or interpreting graphs about the increased rate of economic growth. Typically, they plodded through a list of topics and obscure theories about social behaviour that make up 'the economist's mind', to stand a chance of gaining the prized A grade (or from 2010, the A*) necessary for them to continue with the subject in higher education. As Stanford says, rather than dealing with matters that concern many people, economics has remained an abstract 'technical' subject.

Recent years have also seen the huge proliferation of a variety of Business Studies courses. Concentrating on the internal aspects of running a business, like budgeting, calculating profit margins, marketing techniques and advertising, they rarely involve any sort of real social analysis of organisational power structures. Seen as a 'Mickey Mouse' subject by elite universities (despite their often lavishly funded schools of management), thousands of students – about one in seven – enrol on business related courses every year, particularly in the Million+ clearing universities. With large numbers of these students already having specialised in Business Studies during their upper secondary years or in further education colleges, a 'business studies generation' has grown up. Originally conceived as being 'vocational' alternatives to A-levels, many of these courses are now characterised as 'applied' learning. Adopting more external assessment and more 'book learning', they have become neither vocational nor academic and invariably fail to engage those students already disillusioned with the academic track.

Science is also taught in a valueless vacuum of which environmental education is a subset with all the limitations this imposes. An understanding of environmental problems is thus unlikely to be reached, let alone related to the economy that can no longer be considered separately from the ecology that sustains it. Jonathan Ward broadens this criticism, pointing out that after 30 years of unrestrained and unsustainable economic growth, 'Thatcher's grandchildren' – amongst whom he numbers himself – 'have been soaked in market culture' [and so] 'carry forward a market theory on how to structure life . . . it has engendered responses characterised by notions of the individual, the market, monetary incentives and costing, inequality and a lack of intrinsic non-economic values' (2009: 67). To overcome this, 'Whilst individual learning and teaching is one aspect that is essential, so too is learning as a group and for a group' (83). The curricular reform and reversal of current methods that this implies can be linked to developing democratic control over educational institutions which are recognised as communities of learners and teachers.

An 'education for its own sake'
or one that really matters?

An alternative consensus about basic curriculum principles has not emerged to address not only what students should learn but also how they should learn it. Such an alternative would understand that reinvigorating the curriculum must be as much a political revaluation as a professional project. One that prioritises particular values and conceptions of social justice and sustainability – and as a result cannot be left to teachers and educationalists alone. In addition, active participation in the democratic governance of the institutions in which they work and learn is a principle which invites staff and students to abandon attitudes and expectations associated with the passive consumption of education. While students who have been made dependent upon their teachers may often ask to be 'spoon-fed', they will also acknowledge that this is not what they really want or need. What would they rather be doing than cramming for tests designed to fail the majority while setting unattainable targets for teachers? Ask them!

Many who share our criticisms of the 'standards' or 'quality' agenda and see it as 'dumbing down', would reject an alternative conception of education with sustainable economic literacy related to real employment opportunities. Even though this would encourage students to be 'enquiring, critical and thoughtful' and to develop 'the ability to undertake independent and self-directed learning', just as exam board syllabuses say that they should, this would not be seen as 'education for its own sake'. This ideal returns education to the traditions of liberal humanism that guided it in the past. It can also appeal to students trying to maintain some genuine interest in their studies, often urged on by teachers who advise them to pursue subjects they enjoy, if only because they will probably do best in them.

Liberal humanism especially appeals to academics in the researching universities who are dedicated to following their own scholarly interests and confuse this 'academic freedom' with other freedoms essential to a democratic society, such as freedom of the press, association and expression etc. Special pleading for 'academic freedom' often disguises academic careerism and has contributed to the clear division in universities between researchers and teachers, the latter regarded as a lower form of life. This is encouraged by the recurrent competitive and expensive Research Assessment Exercise/ Research Excellence Framework. Yet, as the Nuffield 14-19 Review (2008) correctly observes, the ideas of 'academic education' have become so dominant politically and culturally it is almost as if they cannot be questioned or discussed. As a consequence, it is generally only vocational qualifications that are thought to need reforming so that they can be made 'as good as' – or as used to be said, enjoy 'parity of esteem' with – the academic ones which still remain 'the gold standard'.

Part of the appeal to teachers of the new Cambridge Pre-U exam, we noted in Chapter 3, is its linear approach to learning, freeing up time currently used in module examinations and retakes. Many HE admissions tutors claim this better prepares students for undergraduate study and a return to this approach might appear attractive, at least in the short run, to teachers ground down by the demands of current assessment requirements. However, a return to the ideals of liberal humanism falls far short of the relevant, democratic and socially useful and ecological learning that we advocate.

Liberal humanism considers learning to be primarily an intrinsic and 'neutral' activity, something that should be valued for its own sake. It is justified because it allows a process of self development rather than being pursued for material gain. But this view also makes other, more controversial assumptions. It is allied to traditional English empiricism that regards the different subject disciplines as exclusive of one another. Each has its own forms, rules and conceptual tools and language which anyone who wants to pursue research or scholarship within a particular field must first Master. As well as divisions of knowledge, this academic tradition also assumes hierarchies of subjects. For example, it tends to disregard 'vocational' learning and, in England in particular, has considered the arts and humanities superior to the technical and the applied. This is not to dispute that committed teachers working in the areas of humanities and English in particular have not over the years been able to develop stimulating learning opportunities. Still, the hierarchies associated with liberal humanism, while continuing to provide the backbone of traditional universities, also maintained the ethos behind the grammar and sixth form curriculum post-1944.

At first enthusiasts for 'real education' – as they present it – may appear to have a point. They share the criticisms we and many others have made of the commodification and commercialisation of schooling which has replaced 'education for its own sake' by an instrumental view of learning as a purely technical process. Like the Victorian Matthew Arnold, they say this results in 'a new philistinism' and to an extent we agree with their defence of traditional culture against what they regard as the anarchy of 'relativism'. This is the view that knowledge, morals and values can never be absolute, but only relative to the individuals or groups who hold them. As we agree, 'post-modern' relativism replaces more general theories of the world by a fragmented and 'deconstructed' conception of knowledge that refuses unitary sense of anything (Robertson: 1994).

It is ironic that this deconstruction came originally from cultural studies because it sidesteps sociological investigations such as those of Pierre Bourdieu in France. From his 1964 study of *French students and their relation to culture*, Bourdieu and his colleagues went on to expose justifications of education and research for their own sake showing how they serve in the *Reproduction* of an elite. In this process Bourdieu's key concept of cultural capital functions as a substitute for money capital. Returning to traditional measures of cultural capital represented by more rigorous exams and rigid disciplines is therefore quite compatible with the free-market in fees advocated by the antique universities. Indeed, advocates of the one usually support the other.

Radical teaching/ critical pedagogy

Of course, as Jones (1983 and 1996) points out and as we document in Chapter 1, the growth of comprehensive schools allowed some aspects of traditional teaching and learning to be reshaped. Teachers used the 'spaces' within the liberal humanist approach to pioneer the new curriculum we described, but they also radically changed the way that more traditional subjects like English were taught. This radical pedagogy emphasised self-development through creative expression, especially in the primary schools. But progressive teachers were also implicitly critical of the underlying philosophical and pedagogic assumptions of liberal humanism. As we recounted briefly in Chapter 1, they emphasised the equal importance of the 'unofficial' knowledge that students brought with them from their communities. In curriculum areas like humanities, they also advocated a new interdisciplinary approach similar to some of the new universities at the time where many of the new graduate teachers had studied. Rather than providing a detailed syllabus, the interdisciplinary courses which emerged, initially in the form of teacher-assessed CSE Mode 3 schemes, were often frameworks. They were constructed around themes on which individual schools were able to develop their own courses. This paralleled well established primary project work as well as radical experiments in independent undergraduate study, for example at the Polytechnic of East London (Robbins 1988).

These new courses enabled teachers to use the 'classroom autonomy' which the post-war reforms had provided them with and the new social studies, women's and peace studies challenged academic conceptions of knowledge. For instance, the new sociology of education referred to in Chapter 1 sought to explore the politics behind the official curriculum. It argued that all knowledge was interest bound and the product of established power structures. Radicals then wanted to replace such 'official knowledge' with knowledge that represented the interests of oppressed groups, such as women's, Black and anti-colonial studies, or studies that looked at the world from a working-class perspective – Paolo Friere's *Pedagogy of the Oppressed*.

The weaknesses and contradictions of the 1970s initiatives have been reviewed in detail elsewhere (Jones 1983) but some of the issues can be addressed briefly here. Though many of the new curriculum initiatives were the products of a variety of teacher networks or working groups and the enthusiasm and the commitment of the classroom progressives cannot be disputed, the understanding and support of those not directly involved in the profession could not be assumed. With some exceptions, the potentially liberating pedagogy of the classroom was not promoted outside school amongst parents and in local communities. 'Progressive education' as it has been termed, remained essentially a 'professional' activity initiated and controlled by teachers in the classroom, rather than being the product of a wider popular agenda.

Nevertheless, today's 'curriculum socialists' consider that, despite the straight-jacket of the standards agenda, it is still possible to introduce controversial issues and to make space for 'socially critical learning' (Wrigley 2006: 99). Just as socially committed teachers in the 1980s brought the year-long struggle between Thatcher and the NUM into their classroom practice and then, a decade later the Gulf war, today teachers working in inner London schools have produced excellent cross-curricula materials about the Vestas dispute on the Isle of Wight. Other radical practitioners (Coultas 2007) have emphasised the need to reconstruct the process of teaching around an oral approach so as to create a more participatory and sensitive atmosphere in classrooms, not only so that students can use their own experiences but also as a way of freeing teachers from the straightjacket of the government's literacy strategy. Rather than the curriculum being 'delivered' from on high, teachers can use their autonomy to work together to promote change from below. Similarly, 'radical pedagogues' in higher education aim to support each other through networks (Canaan 2002).

Radicals take the view that if lessons and learning are organised differently or if more 'controversial issues' were addressed in lessons, then students would be more willing to learn. Education cannot change without recognising the importance of a radical classroom pedagogy, or for that matter without a teacher force committed to a different sort of curriculum to that peddled by government and supported by academic traditionalists; but we would argue that in itself, this is not enough. The energy of individual teachers and lecturers burrowing away in 'their' classrooms needs to be combined with a much greater democratisation of schools, colleges and universities. The increased alienation of young people from learning and their exclusion from any real democratic participation in the running of their institutions will always be at least as important as the immediate relationship with their teachers. This can only be addressed through more wide-ranging reforms.

Rethinking vocationalism

Nowhere are our earlier references to a 'really useful knowledge' more applicable than in 'vocational education'. New Labour, like every other government, said they wanted to improve the status of vocational education, particularly at advanced but non-HE level. This was part of repeated efforts to shore up 'the disappearing middle' of technical labour being deskilled by automation and out-sourcing. The development of 'world class' diplomas was the latest in a long line of vocational initiatives that coincided with increased staying on rates. As we showed, these have foundered, as take up remains in doubt since those students who can, continue to sign up for A-level in large numbers.

Nevertheless, unlike the liberal humanists, the proponents of vocationalism at least emphasise the relevance of 'learning by doing' to everyday life. They have also emphasised that vocational learning can promote a more egalitarian approach, particularly in terms of assessment processes designed to confirm competence rather than student abilities at abstract thinking and that less formal relations between students and teachers can be encouraged. However, as we suggested in Chapter 2, it is questionable whether the new diplomas are relevant to the world of work and whether the type of learning they seek to promote is 'vocational' at all. Government itself now refers to the diplomas as 'applied' or even merely as 'specialist'. Yet, as we argued, the principal (main) learning within the diploma does not even require the learning of workplace skills.

Just as there is a need to end the current academic discipline-dominated curriculum, which – as the 2009 Nuffield Review points out – presents itself as 'general education', there is also a need to rethink vocational learning. It isn't merely a question of improving its status, although an 'overarching' diploma linking vocational and academic education together, in the way the Tomlinson working party suggested, would certainly represent a step forward. The origins of a more general 'critical vocationalism' can be found in the work of the early twentieth century US educationalist John Dewey who in addition to 'trade skills' wanted the inclusion of economics, civics and politics 'to bring the worker in touch with the problems of the day and the various proposals for its improvement' (Dewey 1966: 318). The early nineteenth century English radicals and Chartists also refused to differentiate between 'liberal' and 'practical' education, or 'theoretical' and 'applied' knowledge. As Johnson recorded (1983: 22):

> they included practical skills, but not just those wanted by employers. The list included things like . . . how to make political speeches . . . it taught people what social changes were necessary for real social amelioration.

Introducing a multi-level 'general diploma for everyone' (Allen and Ainley, 2008b), while not precluding 'specialisation' in particular areas and with genuine workplace learning, would at least go some way to breaking down the competitive divisions between learners and between institutions and could point towards the more emancipatory learning associated with Dewey and the early nineteenth century radicals. It could allow the incorporation of other qualifications and be integrated with degree programmes. It could also develop new relationships between institutions, while still leaving them to deliver it in different ways.

'Thick HE'

In Further Education, as Ruth Silver, Principal of Lewisham College, suggested to the House of Commons Select Committee on Education in 2004, at the same time as neighbouring Greenwich and Goldsmiths' undergraduates 'aim higher', why should they not also 'go further' by attending their higher education institutions' partner FE colleges to acquire the practical competences employers always complain are missing in graduates who at best have theoretical 'book knowledge' without practical application? This would combine 'higher' with 'further', education with training and 'deep' with 'surface' learning, or theory with practice. What Silver called 'thick HE' would thus unite practical competence with generalised knowledge. Unfortunately her idea never caught on!

Historically the FE colleges offered a second chance to those failed by academic schooling and supported the economy with the skills needed for working life. The polytechnics, themselves originating in the FE sector, also represented an alternative relation of education to employment very different from the 'finishing school' model of universities at the time. In the best cases the polys combined generalised knowledge with developing skill at work. The positive lessons of the polytechnic experiment should not therefore be lost. Culture could be recreated and craft recovered in new relations of HE to FE and schools. Marx's polytechnic education not being confined to any one trade but applying science to production to 'impart the general principles of all processes of production, and simultaneously initiating the child and young person in the practical use and handling of the elementary instruments of all trades' in 'technical schools (theoretical and practical)' (quoted in Small 2005: 107).

This is a way to rethink that New Labour weasel word 'employability'. Students from FE and the new (new) universities have to convince remaining employers that, while their abstract 'book knowledge' may not be expressed with the literary elegance of the 'Cambridge model essay' (as in Mann 2003), their practical all-round experience has given them the 'nouse' to put that theory into practice. In the long term, the crisis of legitimacy for a competitive education system geared to meeting the 'needs' of a labour market in recession calls into question the continuing separation of the academic from the vocational.

As crucial as the content and organisation of any new curriculum is the way that learning takes place. At the centre of this is the relationship between students and teachers. Creating a real learning society requires us to develop a new consensus between teachers and taught. For education to win back the confidence of young people and be seen as something more than just an increasingly discredited way of collecting credentials for a labour market in which their worth continues to decline, there needs to be a renegotiation of the relationship between teachers and taught, between education 'professionals' and their students in new forms of democracy and participation. In this book we emphasise the continued power and importance of young people being able to drive their own learning but also the new role that teachers and lecturers can play in helping them to achieve this.

The screen generation

If education has reshaped the lives of young people then the arrival of new digital and communication technology has revolutionised them. Recognition of the changing role of ICT is central to any informed discussion about the current lives of young people and society in general. In what is becoming a rerun of the 1970s debate about the cultural effects of television on young people and their relationship with adults (Postman 1983), discussion is typically polarised.

According to some writers, the growth of ICT has contributed to young people having now become 'toxic', caught up in a consumer-driven, sedentary, screen-based lifestyle and a market-driven 'culture of cool' that has undermined their ability to function as proper social beings (eg. Palmer 2006). According to Brighton University Professor Tara Brabazon, quoted in *The Times* (14/01/08), internet search engines are part of the dumbing down process – providing only easy answers to difficult questions. Elsewhere it is assumed that a 'wired' generation cocooned in their bedrooms and spending up to 20 hours a week online (*Guardian* 25/03/08) can only have negative consequences for social integration – Putnam's *Bowling Alone*, only worse.

Of course, with the proliferation of a do-it-yourself IT literacy amongst young people has come the increased power of big business to buy advertising space and manipulate and create consumers. Recognising the lucrative nature of the education market, which has so far remained relatively immune to the economic downturn – as anybody who has attended events like the annual British Education and Training Technology show will be able to testify – ICT companies have been anxious to position themselves as 'innovators' offering exciting new partners for schools, colleges and universities. They are eager to demonstrate how schoolchildren aged from four to 11 can use an array of new 'smart' products to participate in lessons, play games and solve problems in a 'fun' environment. In promoting the way in which hand-held devices allow learning to take place 'anywhere' and in emphasising that new types of communication media are taking over from traditional teaching, the ICT companies present themselves as twentyfirst century 'deschoolers' (Illich 1973). We are not advocating 'deschooling' but we do not deny that the new technologies afford the potential for young people's views and opinions to be heard more easily (Buckingham 2002) and for extraordinary creativity shown by an October 2005 *Guardian/* ICM poll that found a third of 14–21 year olds with internet access had launched their own blog or website and published their own material.

In the current climate however and in the context of the workforce remodelling described in Chapters 1 and 2, there is a danger of a very different future scenario for screen-driven, personalised learning. Instead of students having more control over their learning, a new form of 'teacherless learning' could download mass-distributed, standardised materials to computer terminals, serviced by underqualified and underpaid support staff. They would supervise 'non-academic' students or those with 'behaviour issues' on personalised learning pathways suitably isolated from students on traditional exam programmes.

In the 1970s television was widely seen as threatening the status of 'childhood'. Children were growing up too fast and with the open access allowed by the new media, there were no longer the secrets of print. There were also concerns about how the cultural implications of the new visual media threatened the boundaries between children and adults. There may be a certain irony here in that many of those worried about young people and ICT may also fear the loss of adult power to a generation much more IT literate and invariably better able to use it than themselves. The interactive nature of digital technology can be contrasted with one-way TV. Those concerned about the fragmented modern family household often forget that while adults may spend an evening passively 'viewing', it is youngsters tapping away upstairs (the 10–20 age group also own nearly eight million mobile phones) 'who just can't stop talking to each other'(*Guardian,* 10 November 2009). This has transformed particularly girls' 'bedroom culture'.

Really personal learning

A new consensus about learning would allow young people to use their array of new communication and information processing abilities in conjunction with teachers and lecturers, who as educational professionals would be valued for their skills as 'tutors' or 'facilitators ' able to use their intellectual and pedagogic expertise to create genuine personalised learning for young people. It is reasonable to assume that for those under 16 – or perhaps 14 (ie. primary to middle school) – schooling would still remain a largely formal experience, in non-selective and non-denominational schools admitting students on a nearest first basis – albeit with a greatly reformed and 'really useful' curriculum and a scaled-down assessment culture. Learning for those beyond 14 or 16 however could be combined with learning alongside adults in much more relaxed environments, such as are sometimes provided in FE. Organised through, for example, a network of locally provided 'learning centres'(we borrow the term from the ICT-based 'City Learning Centres', one of the more progressive ideas of New Labour's *Excellence in Cities* programme) into which existing sixth form and FE could be transformed in relation to HE.

As the National Union of Teachers (2005) recognises, proper personalised learning will only become a reality by increasing the amount of 'one-to-one' provision, but also by ensuring that each student has a personal tutor who is a qualified teacher. All personalised programmes of study should include a considerable element of independent study within a framework negotiated with, supported by, or even in collaboration with their tutor. Within this framework, there is no reason why students would not be able to use their expertise and enthusiasm for online sources to 'google up' the evidence.

A personalised programme of learning does not mean that students should always be learning individually. As well as changing the relationship between teachers and taught, learning will always remain an important collective and democratic activity. We would anticipate that in order to gain the sort of 'general diploma' referred to above – as in the long-standing Scottish highers – students would be required to participate actively in a programme of general education through which they could continue to develop a broad range of intellectual interests, including the ability to participate in democratic 'citizenship'. In the spirit of what has been argued above, students – and their tutors for that matter – would be able to collaborate in such 'independent' but also collective study.

Critical space within education for seeding new ideas must be preserved and extended by making scientific research, scholarship and artistic creation an integral part of the independent study of all students, rather than separating teaching from research. This in essence is the answer to the vexed question of research in higher education which has become a shibboleth for many academics clinging to their status as more than teachers. Our position is the opposite – research should be generalised to as many teachers and their students as possible. This is not to deny the necessity also for specialist researchers. While opposing the concentration of research that the state has encouraged over the past 20 years, specialised research – especially big science projects – needs to be sustained through dedicated national or European research institutes and funded accordingly, rather than with contributions from student fees and through competitive bidding. Above all, state-funded research should not be prostituted to commercial interests as is increasingly happening with predictable results.

Localising universities

While often preaching the virtues of democracy and dwelling on their importance to society in general, while ignoring their long history of reliance upon state funding, universities and some of their most liberal academics throw up their hands in horror at the thought of more 'government intervention' in their sector. Yet, as proposed above, it is essential that universities are not allowed to hide behind their 'research ethos' and as we suggested (Allen and Ainley 2007) are brought into local democratic provision with the local community having first call on their extensive resources and facilities. It is a travesty of the current system that it is often some of the newest universities that have the strongest links with local residents.

This would not mean that higher education should necessarily be the direct responsibility of Local Authorities, as the polytechnics and colleges were until 1992/93, but it does imply that HE institutions should play an active part in any new local or regional structures that may be created to plan education for local need (Allen and Ainley 2008). The same approach could be adopted towards private schools which might, at least for the foreseeable future, retain their 'independence' but become mutual institutions, prevented from charging fees and instead enrolling children from the surrounding area, in accordance with principles agreed locally – perhaps for those with special needs requiring intensive residential support. As with universities, their extensive facilities would constitute 'social property' available for community use.

It goes without saying that higher education, as well as further and other adult education, should be free and financed by a sharply progressive income tax rather than a graduate tax as NUS currently advocates. There would also be a restoration of mandatory maintenance grants or the concept of a minimum income for all young people, whether in work, training or education. Real 'widening participation' would also require a change in the way provision was organised and a breakdown of the division between full-time and part-time courses.

Education, democracy and participation

Widening participation, even involving the sorts of learning arrangements that we suggest above, needs to be distinguished from the task of democratising education so that it represents the real interests of young people. The National Union of Teachers, for example, has long been in favour of a 'progressive' curriculum and ardently supports 'child centred' education, but, as Apple and

Beane (1995) note, democratic schools seek not only to reduce the effect of social inequalities but to change the conditions that create them. As well as a more democratic curriculum, a more democratic education system would increase student involvement in governance and it would also ensure students had equal rights as members of the school community. As Hatcher (2008) observes, citizenship is a compulsory subject in the National Curriculum but school students have few active rights as citizens of their schools.

At the same time that New Labour continued to run education in a top-down way with its products distributed through an internal market, government made much of the importance of developing a 'student voice'. While teacher unions have been understandably concerned about a 'consumerist' approach to participation (NUT 2009), there has been little discussion about internal school democracy. Teacher organisations have, as we have suggested here and previously (Allen and Ainley, 2007), operate with a 'professionalist' model. Emphasising the commitment of their members to public service rather than self-gain, they have continued to oppose the encroachments on member's professional autonomy in the classroom, outlined in Chapter 1. The principle of school councils made up of elected student representatives has been supported by teacher organisations, particularly the NUT, but the brief of these councils has been narrow, often limited to consultation about changes to school uniform, for example, not whether there should be a uniform in the first place. Support for school councils and the concept of 'student voice' has also often been justified primarily in educational terms – improving students' confidence to take decisions or as an extension of a school's citizenship education programme. For Wrigley (2006) the 'student voice' project may have the potential to transform power relationships, but, as he admits, 'inserted into an authoritarian system dominated by inspection and top-down control, it could easily have a different result' (67). While research commissioned by School Councils UK in 2007 reported that nearly all schools had a school council, the annual conference of the English Secondary Students' Association (ESSA) recorded that only 8 per cent of students thought that their school council was effective.

At a more formal level and in the context of privatisation,

increased school financial autonomy and 'outsourcing' of services, there is also a need to rethink the role of Local Authorities as agents of local democracy. As we noted, they have changed out of all recognition but there has been little if no discussion about this. One exception is Richard Hatcher's 2002 proposal for establishing Education Forums comprising elected representatives of school communities, including school students and their parents to discuss and take positions on all policy issues and develop a local Education Plan.

Attempts to improve 'student voice' or proposals for changing education governance can be contrasted with the 'democratic schools' described by Apple and Beane (1995) in the USA or the 'citizen school' in Porto Alegre, Brazil (Hatcher 2002). Countersthorpe College in Leicestershire with its staff-student standing committees (Watts 1977) is probably the most radical example of extending school democracy in this country, apart from A.S. and Zoe Neill's Summerhill that Ofsted unsuccessfully attempted to close. Such examples of schools making radical breaks with traditional conceptions of power and authority, while demonstrating what is possible, are generally few and far between and there has been little in the way of blueprints for greater involvement of students at local or national level. The final section of this chapter will therefore return to the issues raised at the end of the previous chapter and address the question of 'agency'.

'All dressed up and nowhere to go', the myth of the lost generation

Media references to 'lost youth' evoke images of young people who have dropped out of education or become socially excluded on the margins of society. For example, 'feral youth' on housing estate street corners, gangs of black youth in South London – in general the 'hard core' NEETs, officially at least not in employment, education or training, who have continued to buck the system and invariably refuse help. During the spring and summer of 2009 however, the term 'lost generation' – used to describe the suffering of young people under Thatcherism (eg. Davies 1997)

– was rehabilitated by the media, politicians and some economists to describe the current plight of successive groups of young people who had become the victims of an economic downturn and a contracting labour market. Initially used to describe a generation of graduates due to leave university but now unable to move into graduate jobs, it became associated with 'betrayal' – a 'young gifted and jobless' (*Independent* 12 August 2009) generation let down by a Labour government (eg. *Daily Express* 13 August 2009); 'Generation Crunch' who feel 'like someone who is suddenly smacked in the face by a friend', having 'dutifully studied for decent degrees, prettified their CVs with useful internships and bounced out of university last summer. The world was their oyster. And then: thud.' (*Guardian* 10 January 2009).

As the summer progressed, 'lost generation' was also applied to thousands of aspiring students unable to obtain places at university, despite passing their A-levels – in some cases with top grades. Many were forced to take an unplanned gap year having been told they had little option but to reapply again the following year. However, by September, career advisory services as well as *The Guardian* (1 September 2009) were providing a more positive take, describing how many young people unsuccessful in the university 'clearing' process were now 'clearing off' to participate in alternative, less expensive but equally challenging ways of using this unexpected free time. Eventually in September, *The Daily Mail* (19 September 2009) returned to an 'underclass' to frighten its readers with 'a generation of violent, illiterate, lawless young men living outside the boundaries of civilised society' and chiming with Tory 'broken Britain' claims. (Both, incidentally, ignoring the way in which 'the lumpen proletariat', as Marx called the 'passively rotting social scum', were reabsorbed during successive upturns and wars – Mann 1991.)

As we said at the end of Chapter 4, recent academic work about the changing nature of 'transition' from youth to adulthood, though not describing young people as 'lost', also raises the question whether young people are any longer able to make the sort of definite transition to adulthood that used to be the norm in the post-war years. Then on the way to adulthood young people passed through the particular stages we described in Chapter 1

– leaving school and starting work, leaving home and getting married and so on. As we noted in Chapter 4, academic theorists claim that young people now have to live in 'risk societies' (Beck 1992) or face 'runaway worlds' (Giddens 1991) where the journey from youth to adulthood is always going be a fractured and uncertain process as a result of the disappearance of 'old certainties', not only class and its associated class cultures but also the weakening of traditional gender ties. As a result, for Giddens, young people living in 'late modernity', as he calls the present day, are increasingly forced to negotiate 'lifestyle choices' (Jones 2009:72). This has become key in the creation of a self-identity. Giddens uses the concept of 'strategies' to describe how individuals navigate their world. In many ways Beck, Giddens and their like, celebrate the collapse of the old passages and pathways of transition. According to Beck, using the language of the existential philosophers, this has resulted in 'forcible emancipation' – a situation where young people have no choice but to face their freedom.

In our view, labelling young people as 'lost' is not only unhelpful and rather patronising but also implies an impending identity crisis. We have pointed out the limitations of the 'post-modern'/ 'late modern' theories about the 'individualisation' of society, even when these are accompanied by an admission that the choices that youth make are still 'constrained' by differences in economic background. 'Strategies' that young people adopt, while they may be 'reflexive' and, perhaps inevitably the product of 'individual biographies', are, we maintain, also the product of the recomposition of the class structure and the changing relationship between education, economy and society. Young people, particularly working-class young people, have always developed 'collective strategies' to respond to their situation in society. The current orientation towards education which we have described as being 'instrumental' or 'alienated' is an example of such a response.

Understanding the difference between 'value in use' and 'value in exchange', many young people are only too aware that the more qualifications you have, the better chance you have in the labour market. The consequence is that, as we have said, they learn what they have to, when they have to and, as we added in Chapter 2, sometimes by whatever means they have to. In many respects, the 'acceptance' of the school regime by the majority of young people would appear to be the complete opposite of the working-class 'lads' described by Paul Willis in the East Midlands in the 1970s and which we referred to in Chapter 1. Willis's 'lads' deprecated their teachers and ignored careers advice. In choosing to 'fail' and follow fathers, neighbours and relatives into manual factory employment, something they considered to be both an assertion of masculinity and also an act of solidarity with their male working-class peers, as well as a defiance of the middleclass (and school) world of the pen pusher, the 'lads' had a clear collective but also a class strategy. As Hatcher (1998) points out, there are however a variety of collective strategies or 'orientations' available to young working-class people in terms of how they perceive school and labour market transition. Willis described one that was particularly distinctive at a particular time but only ever a minority and masculine option.

In many respects, what we refer to as a generation of 'new kinds of students' has more in common with the *Ordinary Kids* studied by Phil Brown in 1987. Rather than dreaming of extensive occupational mobility and 'getting out' of the working class but also – unlike 'the lads' – not rejecting school, these young people, living in a time of greater economic uncertainty, simply wanted to 'get on' in life. As a result, they had to decide whether the immediate disadvantages of having to remain at school were likely to be less than the consequences of leaving at the earliest opportunity and looking for work. The new students today similarly recognise that at the start of the twentyfirst century having a degree is now the norm and provides some security against having a job where 'you have to stand up all day', 'a life working in fast food', 'something better than Sainsbury's jobs' (Allen 2004). In filling in their UCAS application forms and making decisions about where to study they, much like Willis's 'lads', are also 'active choosers' – the term used by Stephen Ball and colleagues to describe the more economically privileged/ middleclass students in their study of post-16 transition paths (Ball et al. 2000). In making individual decisions, they are, as any teacher working in post-16 and dealing with UCAS applicants knows, involved in a collective process, discussing applications and sometimes even synchronising them with their friends.

A major argument of this book is that it is for sections of the 'working middle', rather than for the socially and educationally marginalised 'underclass', that a crisis of legitimacy could become most severe. Often being the first members of their families to have attended university, they are loaded with debt and often still living with their parents. Unless they wish to remain unemployed, they will have to move into the sorts of jobs that, as a result of attending university, they thought they would avoid. As stated in Chapter 4, the current surge in applications for higher education, just like the increase in the number of students wanting to register for postgraduate programmes, while appearing to be the only realistic individual short-term strategy available, can only temporarily mitigate the effects of longer term changes in the relationship between education, qualifications and employment.

This book has described this changing relationship between young people, education and employment. A period of 'jobs without education' was replaced by one of 'training without jobs'. This has been followed by a prolonged period of 'education for employability'. Propelled by the standards agenda in schools and 'widening participation' in HE, it has resulted in a situation where young people are increasingly 'overqualified but underemployed' and where, with the onset of recession, large numbers are without work completely. As a consequence and in terms of their ability to be able to make the transition from youth to adulthood, rather than being 'lost,' many young people know perfectly well where they are but are 'stuck'. Anxious to enter employment, repay student debts and move on with their lives, they are a generation all dressed up but with nowhere to go. It is almost inevitable that the immediate implications of this will be an even greater competition for top grades in examinations and for places in higher education. Of more serious concern in the long term however, is the very real possibility that young people may begin to believe that education has lost its legitimacy as an agent for moving their lives forward into a meaningful and productive adult world.

To confront this situation of growing cynicism and demoralisation, a new kind of education is necessary in which young people can be properly involved in shaping their world. This requires a new kind of education politics. In this country, beyond the tokenistic participation on school and college councils referred to earlier, there has been little formal participation and little input by young people into decisions about the way education is organised. Compared with other countries, for example in France and Greece where students have recently organised – often almost spontaneously – national protests and major demonstrations, there has been little sign of the re-emergence of the student vanguard from the 1960s. There have been ritual occupations of student unions, while in schools there have been walk-outs by pupils in response to changes in the school day, changes in uniform policy and occasionally in support of individual teachers facing disciplinary action. (And for instance in May 2009 in Loughton Essex, pupils walked out of classrooms in protest against cameras recording their lessons.) There were also of course, quickly coordinated demonstrations by school students as part of the wider protests against the invasion of Iraq, as well as the university occupations in 2009 that we mentioned. All these are telling examples of the potential political power of young people. For most young people though the 'politics' of education, discussion about their school or college, the unfairness of particular exams etc., is conducted informally, in corridors or at break times – although the explosion of social networking has given this a broader and more controversial dimension with the emergence of sites like 'ratemyteachers.com' and 'internsanonymous'!

We have described an education system in which the post-war 'professional distance' between teachers, students and parents has been turned into a relation of producers to consumers. To overcome this, we previously proposed a new type of teacher trade unionism (Allen and Ainley 2007) – one which the American education journal *Rethinking Schools* calls 'social justice trade unionism'. In addition to defending members' pay and conditions, this advocates becoming more of a social movement for education and works closely with parents as well as with students.

The National Union of Teachers (NUT) remains historically different from the other English 'sectionalist' classroom teacher unions in continuing to focus on high quality non-selective state education as well as representing the immediate interests of its 250,000 members. This is still a long way from adopting the profile that we consider necessary if the new alliances that are required for a new education system are to be constructed. While continuing to campaign against some of the worst excesses of the standards agenda, particularly SATs and the Academies, NUT rarely considers anything resembling new forms of teacher-student relationships or any alternative conception of democracy and accountability in education beyond bringing back Local Authorities as they once were and no longer are.

The NUT has however formed a 'partnership' with the Universities and College Union (UCU), itself a recent amalgam of two HE unions. Even though at a very embryonic stage, this is a significant step in the right direction. In an industry where several different unions compete for members, it gives a new cross-sectoral dimension to 'professional unity'. There would seem to be huge potential for extending this alliance to include the National Union of Students (NUS). Around 95 per cent of all Students' Unions throughout the country in FE as well as HE are affiliated to NUS, though in the school sector there are no longer equivalents like the National Union of School Students (NUSS) of the 1970s. (The above-mentioned English School Students Association (ESSA) works through current school structures to extend the government's 'student voice' initiative. Under the patronage of the DCSF, its 'semi-official' status puts it at odds with any form of direct action and it has an unclear relationship with the NUS.)

Other organisations working for and on behalf of youth, such as the various youth sections of all political parties, function to recruit new members to the parent organisation. They thus tend to use young people up and spit them out disillusioned with politics if they do not move on to the adult party. Instead, an independent, self-sustaining campaign for youth employment and the restoration of benefits is needed. Like James Lloyd's 2003 *Think Tank for the Student Movement* proposed for the NUS, which also has this 'turn over' problem in its membership, this would provide some permanence as a forum for on-going discussion and debate in alliance with the teacher trade unions and progressive academics. It could begin to thrash out some of the vexed questions that we have raised in this book of the purposes of education, how to meet recession and how to pay for free HE through progressive taxation.

Lost Generation?

Together with their students and other young people, teachers and all who work for and with young people can reclaim, as we have said, if not the professional status that they have lost, then at least their self-respect by also regaining the pedagogical initiative to reassert their expertise.

Steve Sinnott, General Secretary of the National Union of Teachers until his untimely death in 2008, liked to refer to education as 'the great liberator'. In a period when more and more schools, colleges and universities are increasingly fulfilling a 'warehousing' function and acting as a main source of social control, it is time to start making this a reality.

Afterword

December 2009

This book has drawn a line under New Labour's efforts to reconstruct education around the needs of the global economy and to run the free-market/ post-welfare state system introduced by Thatcher better than the Tories. Hopefully we have explained what went wrong, despite the money spent in what will predictably soon be seen as new 'good old days'. We aim to have punctured the national obsession with education which only invites more misdirected effort in future; and in conclusion we indicated the direction for an alternative that must be based on labour market reform instead of attempting to substitute for it.

Continuing economic failure makes this approach more urgent. At the end of 2009, Britain was the only major economic power still officially in recession, hamstrung by its bloated financial sector that was for long celebrated by New Labour as the unstoppable engine of growth. This crisis is increasingly reflected in the education system. Just as the UK has suffered more than most from the 'credit crunch', there has also been a 'credibility crunch' for education as the promises made to young people and their parents have evaporated.

In the last session of Parliament before the general election, promises to help unemployed young people received most media attention in the Queen's speech of 18 November 2009. Similarly, in the December 'Pre-Budget Report', Chancellor Darling announced that everyone under 24 would be guaranteed a job or training after six months rather than 12, with an additional £8 million for 10,000 more graduate internships. He also extended the government's pledge to provide a place in education or training for every 16 or 17 year old.

Budget strategy, however, was aimed more at reducing borrowing and the size of the deficit than boosting jobs. Indeed, Darling's decision to increase the rate of National Insurance contributions for those earning more than £20,000 in 2011 – necessary, he argued, to defend 'front line' services such as schools – was seized on by the Tories as a 'tax on jobs'. Despite the government's huge fiscal stimulus, the economy was shown to have contracted by 4.75 per cent in the year, much worse than the April estimate of 3.5 per cent and illustrating its exposure to the international banking crisis. Many economists also considered the Chancellor's predictions of a 3.5 per cent growth rate by 2011 to be wildly optimistic and that cuts to public services after the next election could result in a 'double-dip' recession and still more unemployment.

According to the Office for National Statistics (ONS), as 2009 ended unemployment was only prevented from reaching three million by over one million people working part-time because they could not find a full-time job. This is the highest figure since records began in 1992. As a result, though the number of those 'in employment' rose, full-time employment fell by nearly 70,000 during the last quarter. The growth of a 'part-time' Britain where over seven million people now rely on part-time jobs, often more than one, has been a major reason why official unemployment and the total number of jobs lost has remained below the level of the last recession, and the rate in the USA, where it has reached ten per cent. This 'underemployment', as Roberts called it, reflects the continuing trend towards a new type of labour force which has lowered its expectations for what used to be considered 'a proper job'. As employers held on to labour by reducing hours, cutting pay and laying off temporarily, government proposed to ameliorate the condition of the long-term unemployed – those unemployed for more than 12 months whose numbers increased by 49,000 over the quarter – by spending £550 million on 'cognitive behaviour therapy' (CBT) to encourage job seekers 'to look for potential solutions rather than the causes of difficulties' (*Guardian.co.uk* 4 April 2009)!

For 18–24 year olds, unemployment increased by 0.9 per cent during the third quarter of 2009, to reach 952,000 or 18.4 per cent of the age group, again the highest figure since records began in 1992. In fact, as we recorded, the number of 'NEETs' – if not the number of officially 'unemployed' youth – had already passed the politically sensitive one million mark. This included 267,000 16–18 year olds who represented 13.4 per cent of the age group (*Guardian.co.uk* 19 November 2009). Graduate unemployment also increased by 44 per cent over the year with reports that 20 per cent of unemployed 18–24 year olds held a degree (*Guardian.co.uk* 21 December 2009). Meanwhile, the Demos think-tank, once influential in presenting progressive policies, proffered the Draconian solution of mandatory 'national service' for young people, arguing that the £450 million needed to fund the scheme could be raised by increasing the rate of interest paid on student loans (www. demos.co.uk)! Business Secretary Lord Mandelson also set out his vision for cuts to further and higher education, stepping up the two year 'fast track' degrees which are already being piloted, and tying colleges and universities ever closer to 'the needs of employers' (Times 24 December 2009).

In schools, the 'standards agenda' is grinding to a halt. Statistics for performance at Level 2 of the National Curriculum – which we reported in Chapter 2 were already faltering – showed that in 885 mainstream primary schools more than half of pupils failed to reach the expected Level four standard in English and maths compared with 798 last year (*Guardian.co.uk* 2 December 2009). The National Association of Head Teachers (NAHT) and the Government continued to search for agreement over the future of SATs, but the NAHT and the National Union of Teachers (NUT) both canvassed members to show 'strong support' for a ballot for a boycott in administering the tests in the summer of 2010 (*TES* 4 December 2009). It was also reported (*Guardian. co.uk* 2 December 2009) that a Steiner school in Hereford, controversially awarded Academy status so as to promote 'diversity' in the state sector, had come bottom in the performance tables after parents refused to allow their children to sit the SATs!

In the absence of anything approaching the necessary strategies outlined in the final chapter of this book and with the polls pointing to a Tory election victory, or at best a 'hung parliament', the prospects for young people and for the state education service are – to put it mildly – not good. In a speech to the free-market Centre for Policy Studies (5 November 2009) Michael Gove, not a member of the ruling Eton clique but nevertheless a rabidly neo-conservative shadow education spokesperson, returned to the Blairite commitment to education as a source of social mobility (see Chapter 3) and argued that it was New Labour's centralisation of the school system that had widened inequalities. Inviting all schools to become Academies, Gove promised 'post-bureaucratic' education with a shift in power away from the 'educational establishment'. What he meant was that the expensive centrally imposed system of targeting would be replaced by a more straight forward market system of competition. To facilitate this, the Tories will encourage local parents and teachers to start 'independent' schools within the state system, akin to the Swedish 'free schools' and Charter Schools in the USA – although the Tories argue that, unlike in Sweden, these schools would not be allowed to make a profit. However, as we also predicted, it is also very possible that some sort of voucher system will be introduced so as to promote greater parental choice as well as greater competition between schools. This could allow the private schools which enjoy charitable non-profit status to contract into the state system, finally finishing it.

Again taking his cue from Scandinavia – this time, Finland – Gove explained that country's high level of performance resulted from teachers coming from the top 10 per cent of graduates. So Gove also promised better qualified teachers and a restoration of their professional status, celebrating the importance of fast-track schemes for top graduates and pledging to give schools more control over teachers' pay and conditions so as to be able to offer incentives to the best staff. This at least offered some future for unemployed graduates, already oversubscribing courses of postgraduate teacher training but otherwise recycled Blair's intention to make every school an independent foundation.

A more typical Tory agenda was promoted by Gove's defence of private schools. It was their 'independence', he declared, not the fact that their fees made them accessible only to a privileged minority that accounted for these schools' academic success. Returning also to traditional Tory concerns with the breakdown of authority, Gove offered a tougher approach to school discipline with no notice detentions and the removal of disruptive students to off-site premises. He promised greater powers for teachers to 'stop and search' and greater protection against allegations from their students. Attacking 'dumbing down', he called for the examination system to be returned to university supervision and supported the expansion and inclusion of qualifications like the International GCSE in league tables. Thus, he argued, data would be much sharper and more 'accountable'. Gove had previously told the Royal Society of Arts (RSA lecture 30 June 2009) that the true purpose of education had become lost with schools becoming more concerned with the social and emotional aspects of child development rather than with teaching and learning.

This led Mathew Taylor, the RSA's Chief Executive and former-Blairite, to claim that the Tories wanted a return to 'chalk and talk' (www.matthewtaylorsblog.com/thersa/an-open-letter-to-michael-gove). Under the Tories, this would only be for the academically able however. For the rest, vocational qualifications would become more practical so that there would no longer be an obligation for schools and colleges to provide the new specialist diplomas, for instance. Instead, Gove reiterated Tory intentions to create a network of separate technical schools.

Gove's endorsement of a new 'diversity' of learning experiences has also been taken up by Edge, an education charity established to 'revolutionise' education. For Edge, a supporter of the Academies programme but also wanting SATs replaced by student profiles, there is too much pressure on young people to go to university (www.edge.co.uk/news 29 November 2009). As with the Tories, one of the ways Edge would raise the status of vocational education with specialist facilities on specialist sites – its *Manifesto* providing current examples from Sweden and Holland. In arguing that 'academic' education has a 'disproportionate influence' within the education system (and in contrast to the arguments in this book), Edge and the Tories are not advocating reform of academic education, only for restricting it to those for whom it is suitable. Considering the structural and historical inequalities that have long been evident in English society, the Edge proposals would only increase the very inequalities that the 'new' Tory Party now officially abhors.

In any case, all these calls for vocational relevance and a return to apprenticeships ignore the fundamental fact to which we have drawn attention in this book that most employers no longer require apprentices. Any employers who do need them run in-house apprenticeship schemes but precious few remain. Automation, deskilling and outsourcing have, we have detailed in this book, laid waste the manual skills base and the same processes are now reaching from what remains of productive industry into the service sector. 'Reskilling' is too often deskilling or at best multi-skilling in generic competences that are represented as so-called 'personal and transferable skills' applicable across a flexible range of employment. 'The demands of employers', like Tesco chief Sir Terry Leahy lambasting a 'woeful' schools system that does not provide young people with the skills Britain's largest supermarket needs, amount to 'paperwork kept to a minimum and instructions simple' (*Daily Mail* 14 October 2009)!

Raising the school leaving age to warehouse young people in schools and colleges is perhaps preferable to preparation for such employment as at least it can keep dreams alive. Certainly, cutting back on post-compulsory education relegates more people to the corrosive consequences of unemployment that are much more expensive in the long term. By contrast, completion of compulsory education with graduation at 18 allied to an assumption of citizenship could help to establish a sense of universal entitlement to post-compulsory education and training. This is contradicted however not only by fees but by the persistence of selective academicism which pitches young people into competition for entry to a hierarchy of universities and courses of study whose social status will soon be directly reflected in their prices. No less than competence-based training, cramming for academic examination reduces the space still available in education at all levels for critical reflection on its purposes. These extend, we have argued, far wider than the common academic default position of 'education for its own sake'. Education is far more important than that!

The purpose of institutionalised learning that must be reasserted, is the critical transmission of the culture to learn from the past in order to discover new knowledge for the future. That education at all levels has failed in this purpose is, we have suggested, the most damning indictment that can be made of its record in the 22 years from the Big Bang in 1986 to the Big Crunch in 2008. Incidentally, this was when the majority of recent and current undergraduates grew up but their 'widening participation' only contributed to exacerbating social disparities in an increasingly unequal society (David 2009).

Meanwhile, Chartered Psychologist, Registered Guidance Practitioner and Author, Denise Taylor offers parents advice in a 2009 guide published by the Department for Business, Innovation and Skills on 'how to motivate not alienate . . . young people who have recently graduated (either this year or last year) or who are planning to work after graduation in 2010'. Putting particular stress on networking and advising four hours dedicated job search per day, as well as volunteering, internships and entry level jobs as 'an interim step', she acknowledges the frustration that is 'a typical response' to 'plans being put on hold' and the prospect of 'earning a lower wage than they imagined'. But 'In a few years the majority of graduates will be doing as well as they always have'.

We doubt very much that this will prove to be the case. For a start, it ignores those displaced by graduates trading down in the jobs market and it assumes resumption of business as usual. Debt goes unmentioned and the tensions of dependent living are glossed over. The renegotiation of relations between the generations and the genders which we have identified as being required, not only by underemployment in part-time working but also by the housing crisis, involves recognition of interdependence rather than the ever-receding goal of transition to an independent identity.

New identifications of self with others and with the world will be required of future generations but education can only help people achieve these if it abandons the individualism and competition it has promoted for so long. Teachers and others who work with young people can contribute to undoing the damage of a market culture rather than sustaining illusions in it, as Taylor urges parents to do. We have suggested that this is the way to regain not only our self-respect but our expertise as teachers.

References

Ainley, P. (1988), *From School to YTS*. Milton Keynes: Open University Press.

Ainley P. (1990), *Vocational Education and Training*. London: Cassell.

Ainley, P. (1991), *Young People Leaving Home*. London: Cassell.

Ainley, P. (1993), *Class and Skill, Changing Divisions of Labour and Knowledge*. London: Cassell.

Ainley, P. (1994), *Degrees of Difference, Higher Education in the 1990s*. London: Lawrence and Wishart.

Ainley, P. (1999), *Learning Policy: Towards a Certified Society*. Basingstoke: Macmillan.

Ainley, P. (2001), 'From a National System Locally Administered to a National System Nationally Administered: The New Leviathan in Education and Training in England', *The Journal of Social Policy*, 30, (3), 457–476.

Ainley, P. (2002), *Monopsony and Mao Tse-Tung, Conversations in Colleges about Learning and Skills Councils*. Unpublished paper to Sixth Annual Conference of the Learning and Skills Research Network, University of Warwick 13 December.

Ainley, P. (ed.) (2008), *'Twenty Years of Schooling . . .' Student Reflections on their Educational Journeys*. London: Society for Research into Higher Education.

Ainley, P. and Bailey, B. (1997), *The Business of Learning, Staff and Student Experiences of Further Education in the 1990s*. London: Cassell.

Ainley, P. and Canaan, J. (2005), 'Critical hope in English higher education today, constraints and possibilities in two new universities', *Teaching in Higher Education*, 10, (4), 435–446.

Ainley, P. and Corney, M. (1990), *Training for the Future, the Rise and Fall of the Manpower Services Commission*. London: Cassell.

Ainley, P. and Weyers, M. (2008), 'The variety of student experience, investigating the complex dynamics of undergraduate learning in Russell and non-Russell universities in England', in J. Canaan and W. Shumar (eds) *Structure and Agency in the Neo-liberal University*. London: Routledge, 131–152.

Allen, M. (1999), 'Labour's business plan for teachers' in *New Labour's Education Policy* (Hillcole Paper). London: Tufnell Press.

Allen, M. (2004), 'The rise and fall of the GNVQ: A study of the changing relationship between young people and vocation qualifications at the start of the 21st century'. (Unpublished PhD thesis. Milton Keynes: The Open University.)

Allen, M. (2007a), 'Learning for Labour: specialist diplomas and 14-19 education', *Forum*, 49, (3), 299–304.

Allen, M (2007b), 'Desperate diplomacy', *Post-16 Educator* (Nov-Dec).

Allen, M. (2008), 'Here comes the Burgerlaureatte!'. *Campaign Teacher*, Spring.

Allen, M. (2008), 'The Pre-U won't do'. *The Teacher magazine*, Secondary and Sixth Form Supplement, Winter.

Allen, M. and Ainley, P. (2007), *Education make you fick, innit? What has gone wrong in England's schools, colleges and universities and how to start putting it right*. London: Tufnell.

Allen, M. and Ainley, P. (2008a), *A New 14+: Vocational Diplomas and the Future of Schools, Colleges and Universities*. Greenwich and Ealing: UCU and NUT.

Allen, M. and Ainley, P. (2008b), 'Why we need a general diploma for everyone'. *Guardian* 15 April 2009.

Anderson M. (1983), 'What is new about the modern family: an historical perspective' in *The Family*, British Society for Population Studies Occasional Paper 31. London: Office of Population Censuses and Statistics.

Apple, M. and Beane, J. (1995), *Democratic Schools*. Alexandra VA: ASCD.

Archer, L., Hutchings, M. and Ross, A. with Leathwood, C., Gilchrist R. and Phillips, D. (2003), *Higher Education and Social Class*. London: RoutledgeFalmer.

Aronowitz, S. (2008), *Against Schooling, for an Education that Matters*. Boulder: Paradigm.

Baker, M. (2009), 'Crunch-time for the diplomas: will they survive?'. *Forum*, 51, (1), 85–91.

Baker, N. (2007), 'The assault on childhood and parenting: why urgent action is needed'. *Education Review*, 20, (1), 38–43.

Baldwin, S. (2008), 'Plagiarism and postmodernism' in P. Ainley (ed.) *'Twenty years of schooling . . . ' Student reflections on their educational journeys*. London: Society for Research into Higher Education.

Ball, S. (2007), *Education PLC: Understanding Private Sector Participation in Public Sector Education*. London: RoutledgeFalmer.

Ball, S. (2008), *The Education Debate*. Bristol: Policy.

Ball, S., Maguire, M. and Macrae, S. (2000), *Choices, Pathways and Transitions Post-16*. London: RoutledgeFalmer.

Barber, M. (1996), *The Learning Game*. London: Gollancz.

Bates, I. (ed.) (1974), *Schooling for the Dole? The New Vocationalism*. London: Macmillan.

Beck, U. (1992), *Risk Society. Towards a New Modernity*. London: Sage.

Beckett, F. (2007), *The Great City Academy Fraud*. London: Continuum.

Benn, C. and Chitty, C. (1996), *Thirty Years On, Is Comprehensive Education Alive and Well or Struggling to Survive?* London: Fulton.

Benn, M. and Millar, F. (2007), *A Comprehensive Future*. London, Compass.

Bernstein, B. (1971), 'Education Cannot Compensate for Society' in B. Cosin, R. Dale, G. Esland and D. Swift (eds) *School and Society*. London: Routledge and Kegan Paul, 110–12.

Blanden, J., Gregg, P. and Machin, S. (2005), 'Intergenerational mobility in Europe and North America'. *Centrepiece*, 10, (1). London: London School of Economics.

Bourdieu, P. (2003), *Firing Back: Against the Tyranny of the Market 2*. New York: The New Press.

Bourdieu, P. and Passeron, J-C. (1977), *Reproduction in Education, Culture and Society*. Trans. R. Nice. London: Sage.

Bourdieu, P. and Passeron, J-C. (1979), *The Inheritors, French Students and their Relation to Culture*. Trans. R. Nice. Chicago: University of Chicago Press (first pub. in French 1964).

Bowles, S. and Gintis, H. (1976), *Schooling in Capitalist America*. New York: Basic Books.

Brennan, J., Osborne, M. and Shah, T. (2009) *What is learned at university? The social and organisational mediation of university (The SOMUL project): Key Findings*. SOMUL Working Paper 5. York: The Higher Education Academy.

Brown, P. (1987), *Schooling Ordinary Kids*. London: Tavistock.

Brown, P., Hesketh, A. and Williams, S. (2004), *The Mismanagement of Talent, Employability and Jobs in the Knowledge Economy*. Oxford: Oxford University Press.

Brown, P. and Lauder, H. (2006), 'Globalisation, knowledge and the myth of the magnet economy'. *Globalisation, Societies and Education*, 4, (1), 25–57.

Brown, P. and Scase, R. (eds) (1991), *Poor Work: Disadvantage and the Division of Labour*. Milton Keynes: Open University Press.

Buckingham, D. (2000), *After the Death of Childhood, Growing Up in the Age of Electronic Media*. Cambridge: Polity.

Burchill, F. (1998), *Five Years of Change: A Survey of Pay, Terms and Conditions in the Further Education Sector Five Years after Incorporation*. London: NATFHE.

Burgess, T. and Pratt, J. (1974), *The Polytechnics: A Report*. London: Pitman.

Butler, R. (1971) *The Art of the Possible: the memoirs of Lord Butler, K.G., C.H.* London: Hamilton.

Cabinet Office (2008), *Getting On, Getting Ahead. A Discussion Paper: Analysing the Trends and Drivers of Social Mobility*. London: Cabinet Office Strategy Unit.

Cabinet Office (2009), *New Opportunities. Fair Chances for the Future*. London: HMSO.

Campaign against Climate Change (2009) *One Million Climate Change Jobs NOW!* London: Campaign against Climate Change.

Canaan, J. (2002), 'Teaching Social Theory in trying times'. *Sociological Research Online*, 6, (4) http://www.socresonline.org.uk/6/4/canaan.html

Carter, M. (1962), *Home, School and Work: A Study of the Education and Employment of Young People in Britain*. Oxford: Pergamon.

Centre for Contemporary Cultural Studies (1981), *Unpopular Education, Schooling and Social Democracy in England since 1945*. London: Hutchinson.

Cheeseman, M. (2009) *Cramming together in the IC*. Talk to Society for Research into Higher Education Student Experience Network day event in the Information Commons of the University of Sheffield 10 September.

Coard, B. (1971), *How the West Indian Child is made Educationally Subnormal in the British School System: The Scandal of the Black Child in Schools in Britain*. London: New Beacon Books.

Coffield, F., Moseley, D., Hall, E. and Ecclestone, K. (2004), *Should we be using Learning Styles? What Research has to say to Practice*. London: Learning and Skills Research Centre.

Cohen, P. (1997), *Rethinking the Youth Question*. Basingstoke: Macmillan.

Collins, R. (1979), *The Rise of the Credential Society*. New York: Academic Press.

Confederation of British Industry (2009) *Stronger together: Businesses and universities in turbulent times*. London: CBI.

Corney, M. (2009), 'Unemployment more appealing than college', *Guardian Further Education* 21 April.

Cote, J. and Bynner, J. (2008), 'Changes in the transition to adulthood in the UK and Canada: the role of structure and agency in emergent adulthood'. *Journal of Youth Studies*, 11, (3), 251–265.

Coultas, V. (2007), *Constructive Talk in Challenging Classrooms*. London: Routledge.

Council of Mortgage Lenders (2008), *July fall in loans to buyers and remortgagors*, press release, August.

Cruddas, J. (2006), 'Neo-classical Labour', *Renewal*, 14 www. renewal.org.uk

Dale, R. (1990), *The TVEI Story*. Milton Keynes: Open University Press.

David, M. (ed.) (2009), *Improving Learning by Widening Participation in Higher Education*. London: Routledge.

Davies, N. (1997), *Dark Heart, The Shocking Truth about Hidden Britain*. London: Chatto and Windus.

DCFS (2008), *Promoting Achievement, Valuing Success, a Strategy for 14-19 Qualifications*. London: DCFS.

Dearing, R. (1997) *Higher education in the learning society*. Summary Report of the National Committee of Inquiry into Higher Education. London: HMSO.

DES (1978), *Special Educational Needs: The Warnock Report*. London: DES.

DfEE (1997), *Excellence in Schools*. London: DfEE.

DfES (2005), *14-19 Education and Skills*. London: DfES.

DfES (2006), *Further Education: Raising Skills Improving Life Chances*. London: DfES.

DfES (2007a), *Raising Expectations, Staying in Education and Training Post-16*. London: DfES.

DfES (2007b), *Making Good Progress*. London: DfES.

Dench, G., Gavron, K. and Young, M. (2006), *The New East End. Kinship Race and Conflict*. London: Profile.

Dennis, N., Henriques, F. and Slaughter, C. (1957), *Coal is our Life*. London: Eyre and Spottiswoode.

Denham, J. (2008), 'Why university participation should expand'. *The Times*, 11 April.

Dewey, J. (1966), *Education and Democracy*. New York: Free Press.

DIUS (2009), *Student Income and Expenditure Survey 2007/8*. London: DIUS.

Dorling, D. (2009), *The Prospects of this Year's School Leavers, Report by Sheffield University for the Prince's Trust*. London: The Prince's Trust.

Dorling, D. (2010), *Injustice: Why Social Inequality Persists*. Bristol: Policy.

Elias, P. and Purcell, K. (2004), *Seven Years On; Graduate Careers in a Changing Labour Market*. London: The Higher Education Careers Services Unit.

Elliott, L. & Atkinson, D. (2007), *Fantasy Island, Waking up to the Incredible Economic, Political and Social Illusions of the Blair Era*. London: Constable.

Equality and Human Rights Commission (2009), *Financial Services Inquiry, Sex Discrimination and Gender Pay Gap Report*. Manchester: EHRC.

Evans, G. (2006), *Educational Failure and Working Class White Children in Britain*. Basingstoke: Palgravemacmillan.

Finn, D. (1987), *Training Without Jobs, New Deals and Broken Promises*. London: Macmillan.

Freire, P. (1996), *Pedagogy of the Oppressed*. Trans. M. Ramos. London: Ramos Press.

Frost, R. (1966), 'The Death of the Hired Man' in *Selected Poems*. Harmondsworth: Penguin.

Furedi, F. (2001), 'You'll always be my baby'. *Times Higher Education Supplement*, 23 March.

Further Education and Curriculum Review and Development Unit (1978), *Experience, Reflection, Learning: Suggestions for Organisers of Schemes of UVP*. London: FECRDU.

Giddens, A. (1991), *Modernity and Self Identity. Self and Society in the Late Modern Age*. Cambridge: Polity.

Giddens, A. (1994), *Beyond Left and Right*. Cambridge: Polity.

Glyn, A. (1985), *A Million Jobs a Year. The Case for Planning Employment*. London: Verso.

Graham, J. (2009) "Their own worst enemies'? A study of African-Caribbean boys.' (Brunel University School of Education: Draft Ed.D. thesis.)

Green, A. (2009), 'Education, Inequality and Erosion of Social Cohesion'. *Forum*, 51, (1), 12–13.

Green, A. and Ainley, P. (1996), 'Education Without Employment: Not meeting the National Education and Training Targets'. *Journal of Vocational Education and Training*, 48, (2), 109–126.

Green, F. and Zhu, Y. (2009), *Overqualification, Job Dissatisfaction and Increasing Dispersion in the Returns to Graduate Education*. Canterbury: University of Kent Department of Economics.

Greenwood, W. (1933 and 1993), *Love on the Dole*. London: Vintage.

Haldane, A. (2009) 'Losing trust in credit, the global financial collapse', *Society Now*, Summer, 14.

Hall, S. and Jefferson, T. (eds) (1976), *Resistance Through Rituals: Youth Sub-Cultures in Post War Britain*. London: Harper Collins.

Hanley, L. (2008), *Estates: An Intimate History*. Cambridge: Granta.

Harari, P. (2005), 'Popular but wrong'. *Radical Education Journal*, 3, 6–7.

Hatcher, R. (1997), 'Class differentiation: rational choices?' *British Journal of Sociology of Education*, 19, (1), 5–24.

Hatcher, R. (2002), 'Participatory democracy and education: the experience of Porto Alegre and Rio Grande do Sul, Brazil'. *Education and Social Justice*, 4, (2), 47–64.

Hatcher, R. (2008), 'Participation and democratisation in the school system'. Unpublished paper to the Education for Liberation Conference, London, June.

Henwood, D. (2003), *After the New Economy*. New York: New Press.

HMSO (1943), *Report of the Committee of the Secondary Schools Examination Council, Curriculum and Examinations in Secondary Schools (The Norwood Report)*. London: HMSO.

HMSO (1963), *Higher Education (the Robbins Report)*. London: HMSO.

Higher Education Funding Council for England (2009), *A Guide to UK Higher Education*. Bristol: HEFCE.

HMSO (1967), *Children and Their Primary Schools (the Plowden Report)*. London: HMSO.

Hobsbawm, E. (1995), *Age of Extremes, The Short Twentieth Century*. London: Abacus.

Illich, I. (1973), *Deschooling Society*. Harmondsworth: Penguin.

Independent Committee of Inquiry into Student Finance (2000), *Student Finance: Fairness for the Future (The Cubie Report)*. Edinburgh: Scottish Executive.

Jackson, B. and Marsden, D. (1962), *Education and the Working Class*. London: Routledge.

Jary, D. (2007), 'The New Higher Education – 10 Years On' in *Proceedings of the Dilemmas in Human Services International Research Conference* (ed.) J.Radcliffe and M.Dent. Stoke: University of Staffordshire.

JMConsulting (2008), *The Sustainability of Learning and Teaching in English Higher Education. A Report prepared for the Financial Sustainability Strategy Group.* London: HEFCE.

John, G. (2006), *Taking a Stand.* Manchester: Gus John Partnership.

Johnson, R. (1983), 'Educational Politics: the old and the new' in A. Wolpe and J. Donald (eds) *Is there anyone here from education?* London: Pluto.

Jones, G. (1995), *Leaving Home.* Milton Keynes: Open University Press.

Jones, G. (2009), *Youth,* Cambridge: Polity.

Jones, G. and Wallace, C. (1992), *Youth, Family and Citizenship.* Buckingham: Open University Press.

Jones, K. (1983), *Beyond Progressive Education.* London: Macmillan.

Jones, K. (1989), *Right Turn,* London: Hutchinson.

Jones, K. (1996), 'Cultural politics and education in the 1990s' in R. Hatcher and K. Jones (eds) *Education After the Conservatives.* Stoke on Trent: Trentham, 1–26.

Jones, K. (2003), *Education in Britain 1944 to the Present.* Cambridge: Polity.

Keeley, G., Burke, J. and Kington, T. (2008), 'After the boomers, meet the children dubbed "baby losers"'. *Observer,* May 11.

Keep, E. (2009), *Employers and the labour market: Key to future progress 14-19.* Contribution to Nuffield review of 14-19 Education and Training in England and Wales Conference 2009 at the London University Institute of Education, 22 September 2009.

Lansley, S. (2009), *Life in the Middle, The Untold Story of Britain's Average Earners.* London: TUC.

Lave, J. & McDermott, R. (2002), 'Estranged (Labor) Learning'. *Outlines,* 1, 19–48.

Lawton, D. and Dufour, B. (1973), *The New Social Studies. A Handbook for Teachers in Primary, Secondary and Further Education.* London: Heinemann.

Leadbeater, C. (1999), *Living on Thin Air: The New Economy.* London: Viking.

Leathwood, C. and Read, B. (2009), *Gender and the Changing Face of Higher Education, a Feminized Future?* Maidenhead: Open

University Press and the Society for Research into Higher Education.

Leitch, S. (2006), *Prosperity for all in a Global Economy – World Class Skills*. London, HM Treasury.

Leys, C. (2001), *Market-Driven Politics, Neoliberal Democracy and the Public Interest*. London: Verso.

Lloyd, J. (2003), *A Proposal for a 'Think Tank' for the Student Movement*. Draft paper. London: NUS.

Lloyd, T. (2009), *Don't bet the house on it*. www.compassonline.org.uk

London Region UCU (No date), *A manifesto for Further Education*. London: UCU.

Lucas, G. (2009), 'Why is "selection" still such a dirty word?', *Times Education Supplement*, 30 January.

Macfarlane, N. (1980), *Education for 16–19 year olds: A Review undertaken for the Government and the Local Authority Associations*. Stanmore: DES.

Mann, C. (2003), 'Summary Report of Findings of the Project on Indicators of Academic Performance'. *Cambridge University Reporter*, 12 February.

Mann, N. (1991), *The Making of an English 'Underclass': The Social Divisions of Welfare and Labour*. Milton Keynes: Open University Press.

Mansell, W. (2007), *Education by Numbers*. London: Politicos.

Martell, G. (1976), 'The Politics of Reading and Writing' in R. Dale, G. Esland and M. MacDonald (eds) *Schooling and Capitalism: A Sociological Reader*. London and Milton Keynes: Routledge and the Open University Press.

Mason, P. (2009), *Meltdown: The End of the Age of Greed*. London: Verso.

McLean, M. and Abbas, A. (2009), 'The "biographical turn" in university sociology teaching: a Bernsteinian analysis'. *Teaching in Higher Education*. Forthcoming.

McRobbie, A. (2009) 'Whatever happened to feminism? Young womanhood under new management' in P. Devine, A. Pearmain and D. Purdy (eds), *Feelbad Britain, How to Make it Better*. London: Lawrence and Wishart.

Marx, K. (1964), 'Estranged labor' in *The Economic and Philosophical Manuscripts of 1844*. New York: International Press.

Misra, M. (2007), 'Minds devoured by dog eat dog' in *Times Higher Education Supplement*, 16 March.

Mizen, P. (2004), *The Changing State of Youth*. Basingstoke: Palgravemacmillan.

NUT (2005), *Breaking down the Barriers*. London: NUT.

NUT (2009), Annual Conference motion *Democracy and Education*. www.teachers.org.uk.

National Youth Employment Council (1974) *Unqualified, Untrained and Unemployed, Report of a Working Party set up by the National Youth Employment Council*, London: HMSO.

Nicholson, L. and Wasoff, F. (1989), *Students' Experience of Private Rented Housing in Edinburgh*. Edinburgh: Edinburgh University Student Accommodation Service.

Nuffield (2008), *Review of 14-19 Education and Training, Issues Paper 10*. London: Nuffield Foundation.

Palmer, S. (2006), *Toxic Childhood: How Modern Life is Damaging our Children and what we can do about it*. London: Orion.

Polanyi, M. (1969), *Personal Knowledge, Towards a Post-critical Philosophy*. Chicago: Chicago University Press.

Postman, N. (1983), *The Disappearance of Childhood*. London: Allen.

Power, S. and Whitty, G. (2009), *Graduating and Graduations within the Middleclass: The Legacy of an Elite Higher Education*. Cardiff: School of Social Sciences Working Paper 118.

Pugsley, L. (2004), *The University Challenge, Higher Education Markets and Social Stratification*. Aldershot: Ashgate.

Putnam, D. (2000), *Bowling Alone: The Collapse and Revival of American Community*. New York: Simon and Schuster.

Quinn, J. (2003), *Powerful Subjects, are Women really taking over the University?* Stoke on Trent: Trentham.

Reay, D., David, M. and Ball, S. (2004), *Degrees of Choice, Social Class, Race and Gender in Higher Education*. Stoke on Trent: Trentham.

Rees, M. (2003) *Our Final Century*. London: Random House.

Rikowski, G. (1999) 'Nietzsche, Marx and Mastery: The Learning unto Death' in P. Ainley and H. Rainbird (eds), *Apprenticeship, Towards a New Paradigm of Learning*. London: Kogan, 62–73.

Robbins, D. (1988), *The Rise of Independent Study, the Politics and Philosophy of an Educational Innovation 1970–87*. Milton Keynes: Open University Press and the Society for Research into Higher Education.

Robbins, D. (1991), *Re-cognising Society: The Work of Pierre Bourdieu*. Buckingham: Open University Press.

Roberts, K. (2001), *Class in Modern Britain*. Basingstoke: Macmillan.

Roberts, K. (2006), *Sociology and the present-day student experience in the UK*. Unpublished paper to Society for Research into Higher Education Student Experience Network day event in London June 10.

Roberts, K. (2009a), *Youth in Transition, Eastern Europe and the West*. Basingstoke: Palgrave Macmillan.

Roberts, K. (2009b), *The Middleclass, the Working Class, and the Expansion of UK Higher Education*. Powerpoint presentation to Society for Research into Higher Education Student Experience Network day event at Manchester Metropolitan University, March 5.

Robertson, D. (1994), *Choosing to Change, Extending Access, Choice and Mobility in Higher Education*. London: Higher Education Quality Council.

Roy, W. (1968), *The Teachers' Union*. London: Schoolmasters' Publications.

Silver, R. (2004), *14-19 Reform: The Challenge to HE*. Presentation to the Higher Education Policy Institute at the House of Commons, June 29.

Simmons, R. (2008), 'Gender, work and identity: a case study from the English further education sector', *Research in Post-Compulsory Education*, 13, (3), 267–279.

Simmons, R. (2009), 'Further education in England and the lost opportunity of the Macfarlane Report', *Journal of Further and Higher Education*, 33, (2), 159–169.

Small, R. (2005), *Marx and Education*. Aldershot: Ashgate.

Smart, C. (1997), 'Wishful thinking and harmful tinkering? Sociological reflections on family policy'. *Journal of Social Policy*, 26, (3), 301–321.

Smith, D. (2005), *On the Margins of Inclusion, Changing Labour Markets and Social Exclusion in London*. Bristol: Policy.

Social Issues Research Centre (2009), *Young People and Financial Independence*. Oxford: SIRC.

Stanford, J. (2008), *Economics for Everyone: A Short Guide to the Economics of Capitalism*. London: Pluto.

Sutton Trust (2009), *London Capital of Private Tuition*. http://www. suttontrust.com/news.asp#a059

Taylor, D. (2009) *Parent Motivators, A parent's guide to helping graduates find work*. London: Department for Business, Innovation and Skills.

Tuesday, R. (2009), *Mummy's Boys Stay Home* http://rubyroom.aol. co.uk/2009/07/27/mummy-s-boys-stay-home

References

Turner, G. (2008), *The Credit Crunch, Housing Bubbles, Globalisation and the Worldwide Economic Crisis*. London: Pluto.

Ward, J. (2009), 'The gap between rhetoric and action in sustainability, Did it begin with Callaghan? A path dependent evolution in English education from 1976–2005 that left a marketised society without the skills to achieve sustainability reforms.' (Unpublished Masters Thesis. University of Stockholm Department of Economic History.)

Warhurst, C., Grugulis, I. and Keep, E. (2004), *The Skills That Matter*. Basingstoke: Palgravemacmillan.

Watts, J. (ed.) (1977), *The Countersthorpe Experience*. London: Allen and Unwin.

Whitfield, D. (2001), *Public Services or Corporate Welfare, Rethinking the Nation State in the Global Economy*. London: Pluto.

Williams, G. and Filippakou, O. (2009), 'Higher education and UK elite formation in the twentieth century'. *Higher Education*. Springer online, 6 May.

Willis, P. (1977), *Learning to Labour: How Working Class Kids get Working Class Jobs*. Aldershot: Saxon House.

Wilmott, P. and Young, M. (1961), *Family and Kinship in East London*. Harmondsworth: Penguin.

Wolf, A. (1994), *Competence-Based Assessment*. Buckingham: Open University Press.

Wolf, A. (2002), *Does Education Matter? Myths about Education and Economic Growth*. London: Penguin.

Wolf, M. (2008), *Proust and the Squid, The Story and Science of the Reading Brain*. Cambridge: Icon.

Wrigley, T. (2006), *Another School is Possible*. London: Bookmarks Trentham.

Young, M. (1958) *The Rise of the Meritocracy: 1870–2023*. Harmondsworth: Penguin.

Young, M. and Whitty, G. (1976), *Explorations in the Politics of School Knowledge*. Nafferton: Driffield.

Index